THE
TROUBLE
WITH
CRUISING

THE TROUBLE WITH CRUISING

Hard Learned Lessons in Small Boats

J.D. SLEIGHTHOLME

NAUTICAL BOOKS
Macmillan London

ISBN 0 333 33009 9

First published in Great Britain 1982 by
NAUTICAL BOOKS
an imprint of Macmillan London Ltd
4 Little Essex Street
London WC2R 3LF

Associated companies throughout the world

Reprinted 1984

Photoset by Rowland Phototypesetting Ltd,
Bury St Edmunds, Suffolk
Printed in Hong Kong

Contents

Photographs are by the author
or from his collection.

Line drawings are by Mike Collins

Introduction

Nothing sharpens your seamanship as effectively as a failed engine, a following wind and a swing bridge about to close.

In case the reader should get the idea that I am incapable of going to sea without being wrecked, dismasted, burnt out, laid flat in a gale, totally lost or run down by a big ship, I hasten to stress that these experiences have been the exceptions that punctuate over forty years of cruising in reasonable comfort and without many other incidents of note.

Misadventure is a fine teacher provided you survive the lessons and learn by them. I began my studies some forty-five years ago in an open boat of leaky antiquity as one of a syndicate of three owners, each having an investment of ten shillings in the thirty bob she cost. That boat dished out instruction like a mobile soup kitchen.

I had a local longshoreman as mentor and the fact that he later sold me a seven-foot flattie for five bob ('You can row her on a dewy lawn, lad'), that was almost too heavy and rotten to lift, didn't lessen my regard for him. He was full of rich aphorisms such as: 'It's not where she looks [points], it's where she *goes* [makes good] that matters', and 'If she's too tired to get through stays, then let her sit on her arse'. In other words, if a boat is too slow in stays to get through the wind, make a sternboard of it. He told me to 'keep my head and bottom dry and the rest would look after itself,' and apropos repairing boats, 'In glue and dust I put my trust; if that don't cure it, putty must'.

What may not be realized is that the boat world of over thirty years ago was still quite a small one and the huge and world-wide boom in yachting of all kinds which has filled every river and harbour to bursting point, with boats of every size, had yet to happen. There were no safety standards other than those handed down, few books and no sailing schools. Nobody bothered much. Boats had no guardrails, distress flares were handed on when the boat was sold and never renewed. But then there were comparatively few of us.

I moved from open boats to bigger seagoing ones without noticing it, mainly by convincing myself that I knew all about sailing larger craft. Then the real lessons began, and as the reader will note a great many of them were due to one thing in particular – the folly of placing too much reliance on an unreliable auxiliary engine.

I spent upwards of ten consecutive years sailing for a living as a skipper or an instructor, much of this time in that lovely old schooner *Hoshi*. It was in the early days of the Island Cruising Club in Salcombe, Devon; today, thirty years after its conception and launching by John Baylay, the ICC is a much respected and highly efficient organization which reveres good seamanship and keeps its fleet in immaculate condition. During its early years, though, about which I write, we were parish-rigged with ancient cotton sails, mainly sisal running rigging and, in *Hoshi* at least, an engine that had driven good engineers to take holy orders.

Faith, hope and an anchor ready at the stemhead were the order of the day. Nowadays I view balmy days and calm seas with a pleasure tempered by cynical resignation, like a wary diner with a four-star menu mentally checking his wallet: prepared to enjoy the pleasures as they come, but with an eye to trouble.

It's not getting into trouble that matters so much as how smartly you can get out of it by your own efforts, because if you never meet trouble, plainly you are not sailing hard enough.

1

Every Sin in
the Book

Do you get experience by having it or do you have to have experience in order to get it? The time was shortly after the war and neither Jim nor I had much experience at all, but the fact seemed to have escaped us, thereby providing the master plan for perhaps half the small-boat emergencies of today. We had heard about a motor ketch on the east coast which had to be delivered to a new owner in Emsworth, Chichester Harbour, and did we want the job for fifty quid? asked our informant.

At that time the yacht delivery market was small and such work as there was went to the scores of ex-naval officers who were mooching around on the loose. They took the cream. We wondered at our good fortune in being offered this job. It was February and one of the coldest winters for years.

Fifty pounds was worth a good deal more in 1948 than today, but it had to cover our running expenses and it was no bonanza. This, coupled with the fact that the boat was a lifeboat conversion not used since before the war, should have made us suspicious. 'She has been specially fitted out for delivery,' we were told. Alarm bells couldn't have warned us more effectively and nowadays I know that a boat is either fitted out for sea or she isn't. There is no such thing as a half-fitout.

We took with us our sleeping bags and oilies, a fairly recent chart or two and an ex-RAF grid compass, plus all the warm clothes we could both wear and carry because it was snowing hard when we began the rail journey to Burnham-on-Crouch. We arrived there after a cold, slow journey just as the early dusk of winter was settling in and although it was no longer snowing there was a bitter wind off the North Sea and the stars had the diamond-sharp twinkle of frost. Neither of us had ever been to Burnham but we found the small boatyard under the seawall which had the ketch in its charge.

1

A ferret-faced man in a red-lead-splashed cloth cap greeted us, which is to say he didn't greet us but stood eyeing us and our appearance with disfavour. Plainly we were not gentlemen. I explained our business.

'I should have been told you were coming,' he grumbled. 'I'm just knocking off. Yon's your dinghy', he added, pointing to a shape in the gloom. He led us up on to the seawall. 'Yon's the boat with the two masts.' He turned and started making off at speed. 'Here, hang on a bit, what about the gear and what about the keys and the engine and so on?' I asked him. 'No keys mate, the engine's been fully overhauled and everything is aboard.' With that he was gone.

We got the dinghy up over the seawall, piled our gear in and launched her. A strong ebb was running, but Jim was a powerful lad and we crabbed out towards our command which was one of the few boats afloat. As we drew nearer I felt my spirits fall. Her lifeboat hull had been raised to form what looked more like a bus shelter; she had a bowsprit with a slack bobstay and her mainmast was raked so far forward that any seagull perching there, and being so minded, could have hit the bowsprit four times out of five.

'This thing's leaking,' said Jim, sloshing his booted feet about. I knew then why my own feet had been growing colder by the minute.

We went aboard. I shone my torch down the companionway and saw that the bilgewater was over the cabin sole. We looked at the windows and tongue-and-groove cabin planking streaming with condensation; took in the galley with a frying pan wearing a fur coat of 1939 mould and decided that the frying pan at least was better off than we were. Why we didn't turn and run I shall never know, but we stayed. An hour later we had pumped her out and Jim had given the ancient converted lorry engine a run (it started with suspicious ease) while I found and lit a rusty hurricane lamp and nosed around in the lockers. Then we bailed out the dinghy and went ashore to a pub where we ate hot meat pies and drank ale in front of the fire until closing time.

We had a miserable night. The bunks were soaking and the chill was profound but we were young, fit and fanatical about boats. The ebb down river would end by about 9.00 a.m. and so we had to be up and away before it was properly light next morning. We had no problem about waking up. We were glad of the excuse to quit our clammy bags. While I coaxed an old Primus stove under the frying pan, Jim ran the engine warm and left it ticking over quietly until we had eaten our hasty and nasty breakfast. Then we hoisted the

mainsail and the jib, let go the mooring and banged the engine ahead.
It began to snow.

The road to the sea out of Burnham is long and mainly straight,
flanked by marsh which falls away as the river widens until the
channel runs buoyed between a huge expanse of shoal and sandbank.
At long last you reach the Whittaker beacon where, should you be
bound to the south as we were, you are faced with the complex
business of threading a way through the swatchways that link the
main channels as they converge on the mouth of the Thames.

We were glad of our ex-RAF grid compass, despite the fact that we
used it in its wooden box lodged as near fore-and-aft as we could get
it and ignorant of any possible deviation. The ship's compass had
long since lost its fluid and the card in the bowl lay motionless as a
dead crow in a chimney. The ship had an old Walker log but one spin
of the flywheel (it ground and grated to a halt after a very few
revolutions) convinced us that it was better left in its box. There was
no handlead but there was a window sash weight and a length of
codline as a substitute. Under every sail we could set and, carrying
the young flood with us, we dog-legged from buoy to buoy, through
the Gat, across the Barrow, past Knock John and over Black Deep
where the wind fell lighter, wavered and began to back southerly.

There was little traffic to be seen and it was numbingly cold. By
that time we had rigged tiller lines and led them below where we sat
one either side of the cabin table, holding a line each and steering by
the compass which we had lined up with the centre crack of the table.
Now and then we would stick a head out for a look around. 'To me,'
Jim would say; 'To me,' I would echo moments later. We looked like
a couple of monks meditating over a sacred relic, which was more or
less true.

It was mid-afternoon by the time we had emerged from the North
Edinburgh Channel; late afternoon and dusk before we had the flash
of the Tongue Lightvessel astern and North Foreland away on our
starboard beam. We lighted the navigation oil lamps, hung them in
the rigging and settled to one of the longest nights of my life. At first
we worked two-hour watches but later we found that one hour was
plenty as the wind freshened to southerly force 4–5.

We shortened her down all round with a reef in the mainsail, then
we hove her to while we got the dinghy alongside and bailed it out.
This had been going on at intervals all day and we had hoped and
expected her to take up as the planking swelled. All she had taken up
was time and trouble. We came hard on the wind on starboard tack

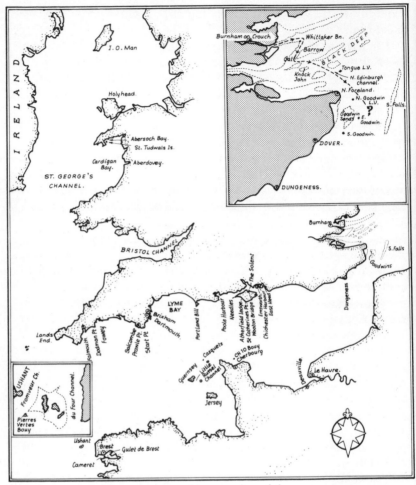

Places mentioned in a number of chapters

with the ebb now against us and visibility falling rapidly. We saw the North Goodwin Lightvessel and then we saw no lights at all.

My DR was suspect in any case. We had only now sailed our charge closehauled and I had no idea of her leeway which I couldn't even estimate now that it was dark. I had a rudimentary idea of offsetting for tide but no log and an uncertain compass. Thus armed I laid a course across-Channel, a course which owed about as much to science as the flight of Wee Willie Winkie. The tide was lee-going but the seas were short and lumpy and we lurched and banged along at a painfully slow rate. Yet it was plain that the old thing had all the sail

4

she could manage, for she was heeling hard down when she wasn't rolling her guts out. Then the mizzen, which hadn't been doing much work anyway, suddenly split up the middle. We stowed it and plugged on under reefed mainsail, staysail and jib, until with a mighty threshing and clattering the jib followed the mizzen. The sails were old, ripe cotton throw-outs from some old, ripe and forgotten boat long since broken up.

That was the way with old cotton sails. The Terylene and Dacron materials of today don't last forever either, but they don't suffer fungal rot. From a new cotton sail, stretched carefully and never stowed when it was damp, let alone soaking wet, you could get many years of good service. However, once it became a bit dodgy it could never be allowed to flog or it was only a matter of time before it simply disintegrated. All our sails had reached that state. We debated starting the engine but we didn't quite know how much petrol the tank in the after locker held and neither did we know how much per hour the engine used. It seemed wiser to lumber on under sail for as long as we could.

It had been around eight o'clock in the evening when we had seen the North Goodwin distant some four miles dead to windward and in the now heavy rain we lost its light soon enough. With the soaked chart sliding about on the saloon table and working one-handed by torchlight, I laid off an estimated course made good which, even allowing for foul tide and leeway, must have been absurdly optimistic. The hours crawled by. Under mainsail and staysail the old boat had heavy lee helm which must have caused even more loss of ground to leeward.

Off watch we dozed fitfully in the lee berth, listening to the rush and slosh of water in the bilges (we were pumping half-hourly), the thump and dash of spray, and the racket of wind and rigging overall. It was the sort of half-sleep you often get in boats when nightmares abound and the sounds of wind and water create muffled human voices, half-dreamed snatches of conversation, a mish-mash of hallucination and tiredness. Then your watch-mate would be standing and dripping on you, shaking you properly awake and another miserable hour at the helm lay ahead.

I came on at midnight and Jim helped me put the ship about. Again and again we tried tacking her but she just wouldn't go through stays, falling astern each time and laying back on her old course. In the end we had to gybe her round and even that took one hell of a long while and occupied a lot of searoom – a fact that had great significance later on. We had a brew of coffee and Jim began his watch below at around 1.00 a.m. after I had laid off a new course from a highly speculative position.

Despite the misery of the night I felt a new confidence as I sailed. The earlier starboard tack had, I thought, taken us well over towards the South Falls and the port tack, with the tide soon to run fair under our lee, was allowing us to point up nicely for the South Goodwin Lightvessel. Like a pig in a tramcar it was! I should have remembered what Les Warman, the fisherman mentor of my boyhood, had to say about pointing closehauled. 'She *looks* but she won't *go* there', Les would say, by which he meant that while your bows may have been pointing up sharply, the course made good is something quite different.

Jim took over, then I relieved him; then Jim again, and at five o'clock in the morning, now utterly weary, I took over yet again. It was still pretty dark and still raining. We had sighted the odd ship during the night but always her lights had been muzzy and not seen until within a mile or less of us, so I had not been unduly alarmed at not seeing the South Goodwin just yet – which was a pity.

The sea had become very disturbed with the wind against the tide and so I was not aware that it had changed its character. Only that more wave tops were breaking aboard and the motion had become heavier, all of which I ascribed to the weather-going tide. Now I slowly noticed a new sound. It was like a sound imagined, or felt, rather than heard, but real nonetheless: a deep, deep undertone like a rumble and heard *through* rather than above the wind. It was, as I have said, pretty dark and yet quite suddenly I saw something ahead and to leeward.

It was a paleness lying in a horizontal line. Then the paleness became plainer and my heart lurched with sudden suspicion. 'Jim!' I called urgently down the companionway, 'come up Jim, come up here, *quick!*' He was dull with sleep of sorts but then he saw it too and snapped wide awake. 'Engine?' 'Yes, mate, and quick!' The engine would not start. There was no electric starter and Jim swung and swung in desperation. It stuttered and died, stuttered again.

I am no engineer and I have now forgotten which part had to be dismantled. Jim had served the war as a mechanic in an RAF Sea Rescue boat and I thanked God for it. But, whatever he took off – distributor cap, fuel filter or what have you – he worked with concentration and singleminded speed. I held the torch and steered, pinching up, watching the line of booming whiteness that now stretched almost parallel to our heading – almost parallel but not quite, because we were closing on it all the time.

Then Jim dropped some small component. Perhaps it was only half a minute before he found it, searching with the torch on his knees, but it seemed an unbearable eternity and I clenched my mouth shut to stop myself from telling him to hurry, hurry. The temptation was to try to tack, knowing full well that she would never get through the eye of the wind and that the wasted time would be fatal. Neither dared I attempt to gybe her round, which would mean paying off and steering towards the breaking shallows. I don't know how far we were from that part of the Goodwin Sands. One hundred yards? It could have been further, but it seemed much less.

Then the engine roared and I yelled with relief as I thrust on the gear lever to get her round in case it failed again. It kept going, however, and with the throttle wide open we swung in a burst of spray, and with the grid compass on a reciprocal heading and the sails drawing full, we hammered and slammed seawards. We were not out of trouble yet, though, and our relief was short-lived. It was the first time we had run the engine flat out and kept it flat out and so we had no idea of the danger that lay in the after locker. Perhaps twenty minutes went by when Jim called out above the roar of the engine. He was pointing and gesticulating at something behind me, then he slammed the throttle shut. 'Fire!!' he said, and he was shouting.

There was a volume of smoke pouring from the edges of the after cockpit lid and the smoke was lit by a flicker of yellow. *The petrol tank was in that same locker*. There was a fire extinguisher of the old-fashioned pump-action type on the bulkhead and Jim was down and back with it in seconds. He aimed it at the locker as I yanked open the lid halfway. Flame licked out. I slammed it shut again instantly, though, because Jim's fire extinguisher was empty, dead. He plunged an arm into a seat locker where we had thrown the deck bucket after bailing out the dinghy earlier and this time when I opened the locker two gallons of seawater thrown with the force of fear put out the blaze in one shot.

I cut the engine. Then we saw the criminally stupid mistake committed by that boatyard when they had 'fitted her out' for the passage. The engine cooling water had a separate outlet below the exhaust outlet and the exhaust pipe itself was *dry* and not even asbestos-lagged! Worse still, the locker had been packed with all the odds and ends of old rope that belonged to that sorry old wreck. Our flat-out burst of speed had naturally heated the exhaust to the point when the rope had charred and then begun to burn. With the long cylindrical fuel tank only inches above the fire, it would have taken a very few more minutes before it exploded. We would most probably have died before we knew what had happened.

It took a long time, the rest of the daylight, but eventually we reached Dover Harbour where we stayed for the following three days, now content to forget our profits on the trip in the luxury of quiet and some comfort of sorts. We sorted the boat out and with the aid of the Primus dried her out a bit below. We ate three big meals a day at a little cafe and slept solidly between times. One day I phoned the owner and told him of our plight but he was unmoved. 'Well, yes, but when do you reckon you'll be able to get my boat here? I've arranged to go fishing at the weekend.' I slammed the phone down!

The weather improved and the wind went northerly, with even a touch of easting in it, fresh and cold but as fair as we could wish. Even the sun came out for us. We got to sea in a hurry and laid a course to clear Dungeness – which was where our final treat lay in store. The dinghy was towing astern on twin painters both attached to the ringbolt in her stem and we had caulked her worst seams with soap, softened overnight in a tobacco tin with a drop of water – an effective treatment learned from Les Warman.

We reached the overfalls of Dungeness and the fun began. Nobody in their right mind tows a dinghy through offshore overfalls or even on a run in anything of a following sea if it can be avoided. But we had neither the experience to forsee the trouble nor the choice of an alternative. The old bitch was wave-surfing in the following seas, which is to say she was alternately wallowing in the trough buoyant as a dumpling then bustling along bows-down and transom in the air in a great commotion of wave crest, foam and fuss, with the rudder shuddering as if at some private revulsion. The dinghy meanwhile, having hung back shyly while we were surfing, would come thundering after us as we lay dormant in the trough and attempt to rape us. Time and again it slammed into our stern or overtook on the inside lane as if some insane trophy were at stake. Eventually we tried tailing extra scope on to the two painters and that did the trick; thereafter we had peace.

The dinghy ran up on us just once more and missed. 'Right you bastards,' it seemed to say, 'try picking the cherries out of this then.' It dropped astern as we surged forwards to bring up with a twang that shook our socks down, then it repeated the trick. Just once. The twin painters held; the ringbolt held; the stem and breasthook remained united but the rest of the dinghy fell astern, awash to its thwarts.

Nothing very much happened on the remainder of that passage. Perhaps we had some trouble finding and rounding the Owers Lightvessel. It would have been surprising if we had not, for my navigation had about it the random quality of a fruit machine with survival as the jackpot. In the light of later experience, we had no business to survive, although at the time I was too busy calling God to witness the state of that awful boat to take much stock of my own shortcomings.

The new owner was waiting to greet us as we chugged up the Emsworth Channel on the tide. Clambering aboard, he looked around at the torn sails, the fire-blackened white paint around the after locker and the twin painters with the stem of the dinghy still attached. We had left it like that as proof and his great flabby chin shook with fury.

Conclusions

That we were totally irresponsible and ignorant is beyond any question. In mitigation I might plead that we had both spent our pre-war years knocking around with boats on the foreshore on the Isle of Wight in an intensely boaty community. It was less a case of big-headedness than of knowing how little we knew or how much one needs to know in order to deliver an unknown and very bad boat around the coast on a winter passage. We were also young and saw problems only when we fell over them. A good seaman can sail almost anything to almost anywhere as the many wartime survivals and escapes had proved. Many, many more escapees in equally unsuitable craft had never lived to tell the tale.

It is easy to lay the blame on the boat. A seaman – a good delivery skipper, for instance – takes a long, hard look at the boat, her gear and her installations before he ever leaves harbour and we did none of those things. In any case, the craftsman never blames his tools. There was and still is a certain honesty about those leaky old lifeboat conversions and the terrible sheds and top-heavy additions built like an elephant's howdah above their original sea-kindly hulls. They are bad and it should take no expert to see as much. They are honest in that sense, just as there are a few gleaming but cheap-skate glassfibre boats on the new boat market that are dishonest – and the more dangerous because of their glitter and gleam.

There are some splendid lifeboat conversions to be seen and also conversions of all sorts of other craft, but in every case the man who converted them kept in mind the original purpose and function of the hull. A concrete keel, a cabin and a set of sails don't make an old harbour launch into an ocean cruiser. There are some fine compromises and some right pigs as well. Bill Smart, founder and one-time editor of *Yachts and Yachting*, for whom I worked for twelve years, was the master of the cryptic comment and of a book published by the rival *Yachting Monthly* about converting lifeboats and titled *Lifeboat Into Yacht* he said, 'Huh. Lifeboat into yacht? Yachtsman into lifeboat, more like it!'

Just after the war there were some amazing bargains to be bought secondhand. There were old hulls which had been laid up throughout the war in mudberths and rotten and neglected, while their sails and gear, still in pristine condition, lay in some loft. There were hulls with rotten topsides but sound below mud level and with lead keels worth a hundred pounds a ton on the scrap-metal market. Hulls without gear and gear without hulls, plus a great mass of ex-naval and other service craft. Hence one saw cruisers whose lead keel had been sold to finance restoration, with a concrete keel as substitute and floating high as a dead dog, lolling around to the least puff of wind. The Lifeboat Service will tell you all about amazing bargains and the amazing number of people who have to be rescued from them. Old, banged-out, leaky boats may be the poor man's road to ownership, and I have owned my share of them. What one must never do is actually go to sea in them.

The half-fitout can be fatal, but at the time I obviously did not attach as much of our trouble to that cause as I should have done because in later years I committed the same error. The yacht lay in a mud berth in Falmouth, where she had lain for a number of years, and three of us were sent from Salcombe to get her ready for a short coastwise passage back to Salcombe where she could be properly dealt with. She was a ketch of about forty-five feet overall and an old boat, wooden but sound enough.

We went flat out at it for a full week, taking great care over what seemed the essentials – sails, rigging, engine, pumps and so on. When I finally declared her ready for sea I was aware of one major weakness, but the weather had been calm and settled with good prospect of the anti-cyclone remaining with us. Moreover, such little wind as there was would give her a run on the *starboard* gybe and this was very important. The major weakness was a patch of rot in the port crosstree but, I consoled myself, this would be the lee one and the engine could be used should a run on the port gybe become necessary.

We had sailed round in the Brixham trawler *Provident*, which we used as a floating workshop, and a delivery crew came from Salcombe to sail the other ketch back. I explained about the crosstree and they agreed to nurse it, then we departed in *Provident* ahead of them. They sailed the following day – at least, they motored because the wind was very light and as expected it gave them a starboard gybe outside the harbour. There was a rumble of thunder.

The thunder squall came from nowhere, striking them on the *port* quarter with terrifying force and blinding rain, causing them to fall flat on their beam-ends and to round up suddenly. There came a crack from aloft and the upper half of the mainmast, bending absurdly for a second, snapped off and went overboard in a wild tangle of trailing rope and wire. The engine was still in gear and a trailing rope went round the propeller while people were still too shocked to remember to throw it into neutral. The squall passed, to be replaced by a strong shift of wind that put them in danger of a rocky and precipitous lee shore. The whole thing ended with the lifeboat being called out and a tow back to Falmouth.

A winter passage features in another tale in this collection (Pure Thoughts and Cold Showers), but the big difference between the two stories is that while one took place in a large yacht under expert management, the one under discussion was the exact opposite. It concerned a small bad boat, weakly crewed and poorly navigated, and what happened is probably closer to the majority of incidents that occur among yachts. In a great many cases the culprits are either sea anglers in ancient motor cruisers or new owners taking delivery of their boats very early in the season – an Easter weekend, perhaps?

Our leaky hull was not a direct cause of trouble although it might well have been a portent of more serious difficulties. Any boat can spring a leak. Some are annoyance leaks like stern gland trickles, but relatively unimportant, while others may be equally slight but potentially dangerous. If there is any water in the bilges of a boat you must know where it has come from. There are few boats that don't have *some* water in them, whether from the stern gland or from a cockpit locker, the chain locker or a leaky skin fitting. Skin fittings should never leak and if they do they need maintenance, because the trickle may indicate something more serious such as electrolytic corrosion of the holding bolts.

Even slow leaks, if left unattended for long periods, such as when a boat is laid up afloat, can be disastrous and I have heard of two yachts which sank when they became so low in the water that a sink waste-pipe, or some such, began to siphon back. To be able to live with a leak we must know whether it is salt water or rain water (even a fresh-water tank leak) and then either deal with it or sell the boat ashore during a drought.

Our makeshift compass is good head-wagging material although I would hate to make a bet on just how many brand-new and well-equipped yachts go to sea with their compasses just stuck on the cockpit bulkhead like a house martin's nest, unchecked, neither adjusted nor even swung. On short buoy-to-buoy courses we can get away with big errors without noticing them. The next buoy a couple of miles away just happens to come up fine to port instead of to starboard – maybe a ten-degree error, but that means being five miles out in thirty which, plus leeway and a stronger tidal set than allowed for, can begin to add up to a surprising landfall. Like leaks, what matters is *knowing* how much and why and then either allowing for or curing the trouble.

That our leeway was spectacular is all too plain, but once again, if you have leeway – and every boat has some – you have to know how much and whether it varies. We could have gained some idea by coming hard on the wind while it was still daylight so that we could take a rough bearing of our wake relative to our course set. At that stage in life, though, I probably wouldn't have realized that leeway in sheltered water can be very different from the leeway made when a fat old boat is lurching and humping her way to windward at slow speed. We were probably making good a course at forty-five degrees to leeward of our heading – 'she won't go where she looks.'

I shall never know the exact part of the Goodwin Sands we almost hit but the flood was well made by then and we must have passed over an outer shoal (maybe the Goodwin Knoll?) and perhaps come close to a patch which is shown as drying nearly two metres. Our luck was phenomenal. Were we too close to have gybed her round? Maybe not, but was the bank steep-to or shoaling? That I shall never know either, and sure as hell I never want to be close enough again to find out.

Our fire, like all fires, need not have happened. The small yard (long since gone) did a stupid thing, but an experienced delivery skipper would have discovered the state of the exhaust pipe before sailing. The one thing that I did right was to shut the locker lid again the instant we found that our fire extinguisher was useless, thereby excluding the air, because it must have taken Jim at least thirty seconds to find and fill then throw his bucket of water. Thirty seconds would have been the time it would take for the fire to get completely out of control.

You rarely see hard-construction dinghies being towed nowadays, but it is due to the advent of the inflatable rather than to the bitter lessons learned. Time was when any yacht too small to take her dinghy on deck had to tow it astern and people knew full well that a strong chance existed that some day they'd lose it. The recommended method of towing was to have the towing eye low down on the stem and the length of tow long enough to allow the dinghy to ride the advancing face of one of the stern waves. In a following sea the scope could be increased to perhaps thirty metres or more and a length of rope secured to the stern of the dinghy streamed astern to check her rushes.

Dinghies in a following sea tend to rush forward, slow, swing aside and then be yanked straight again with great force. They can also become half-swamped with rain or spray which makes them even more pig-headed, and heaving-to to bail them out alongside is both dangerous and bad for your topsides. A tow astern during a quiet local weekend cruise is one thing (even that can be troublesome), but towing on a sea passage is bad news. Even towing an inflatable is troublesome, no matter how tight up to the stern you have it. But if we must tow it, the outboard should never be left in it, nor the paddles or anything left aboard.

2

One Ship,
One Skipper

Her deck-saloon-cum-wheelhouse was the sort of glass construction you find on seaside esplanades where bed-and-breakfast holiday-makers sit to munch fish-paste sandwiches and look at the rain. She had a steering wheel that ought to have had a clock or barometer in the middle of it and her twin Handybillies popped away with a sound like porridge on the simmer. She slept two aft in comfort, two forward indelicately and me on a ledge in the wheelhouse like a house martin. I was her skipper on charter for one month.

The first charter was a walkover because the party knew less about boats than Genghis Khan knew about Mothercare – apart from one day with a Friend of the Family who *knew about boats*, but that is another story.

The second and fateful charter was in Chichester Harbour; it was supposed to be of one week's duration but it lasted about five hours. The charterer was a retired Royal Naval commander with his wife and child and all they had in mind was day cruising with the occasional night on board – nothing exacting or exciting or bearing remotely on danger and discomfort. The weather was warm and settled, hot and windless, so what could possibly go wrong? If I had studied the portents, read the sheep's entrails or even reckoned on Sod's Law, I would have known that such conditions are ripe with potential.

It was the top of the big spring tides and we popped down harbour a little before high water, bound for the Thorney Channel and a jolly picnic. Motoring over the shimmer of glassy water we swung to starboard past the big marker beacons guarding the Thorney entrance with our dinghy astern and our wake fanning out to hiss softly through the marram grass, then we anchored off West Thorney for tea. We sat on deck in the hot sunshine and watched the tide brim higher and higher until the saltings were hidden and the big fat muddy bubbles rode by. The whole wide marshscape lay full and

14

tranquil around us. We poured another cup all round and ate Lyon's jam roll. I was about to learn a valuable if traumatic lesson.

Remembering my role as skipper and hired help, I offered to wash up the cups. After all, I reasoned, my charterer was a naval officer and therefore knew all about charts and suchlike. It never occurred to me that there are naval officers who pilot an office desk and who have forgotten most of the stuff they learned about small boats as cadets. The way out of Thorney was quite clearly marked, even if by then the saltings were completely covered and the entrance beacons were inconspicuously small. The chart showed the channel as plainly as it showed the row of now-covered pilings that flanked the edge of the saltings. We got under way with the Commander on the helm and me below, blowing down the teapot spout.

We were going along nicely when it happened. Suddenly there was a deafening wooden bang and I found myself on my back. The bows went up . . . then down in a shuddering, grinding lurch as the stern rose then fell.

I bounded on deck clutching the teapot. The Commander and I gaped at one another, mouths opening and closing, then we both began yelling at once. Dead astern there showed briefly the raw yellow pine of a propeller-chewed stump. I shot below to sound the pumpwell but I was saved that trouble as from beneath the saloon carpet there came a gurgling stream of oily water. There was a belt-driven bilge pump on the engine, and ripping open a hatch I slammed it into action but almost simultaneously the twin flywheels sent up twin sprays of foulness that oiled the belt which began to slip. The pump stopped.

'Hand pump!' Luckily I had stripped it down only the day before. I wagged the handle at the speed of light but still the carpet floated. The Commander's wife joined me with a bucket. We were floundering around down there like a comic whitewash act in pantomime but still the water rose.

The Commander was on the wheel and aiming for the other side of the river and a scrap of beach. 'Keep calm, keep calm!' he was howling as he rolled an eye over our slithering activities. Then . . . 'Dora, get aft and *pack the bag.*' We had bottled our panic by this time and we were all hard at it being British. I was tempted to dress for dinner. Dora went aft, up and then down via the wheelhouse and began hurling clothes into a big suitcase. I nipped up for a quick look around.

With both engines flat out, the porridge boiled like Etna. The

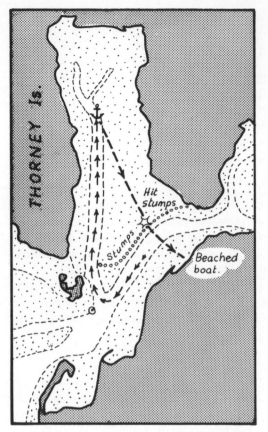

THORNEY Is.

Hit
stumps

Stumps

Beached
boat.

Thorney Channel with tracks good and bad!

inrush of water seemed to have diminished, although I knew this was an illusion. The Commander, white-knuckled and grim of jaw, gripped that absurd toy steering wheel in a 'they shall not have the flag, boys' attitude, but our finest moment was yet to come.

If there is a *Guinness Book of Records* entry for packing a suitcase, Dora has it staked down. Up from below she came, lugging it, while we and the lad watched pop-eyed. 'Get it in the dinghy – the dinghy, woman!' the Commander bellowed, seeing her hesitate. I was due back at the pump but I watched in fascination. She lugged it aft along the side deck and set it down on the narrow stern deck. She pulled in the dinghy by the painter until it had its stem nuzzling our transom. Now then, it needed two hands to hold the dinghy and it also needed two hands to lift the suitcase. I should have rushed aft but I couldn't

16

believe anybody could be that dumb.

She let go of the dinghy and in one smooth flowing movement grabbed and flung the suitcase.

It went bobbing astern on the wake of our frenzied passage, its lid gagging on one pyjama leg like some strange creature of the deep surfacing for a quick snack, then it wallowed, burst open and disgorged its wealth.

A few minutes later we drove shuddering up the beach and our stern sank in the shallows.

Conclusions

Everybody knows that a skipper is responsible for the safety of ship and crew and he either handles everything himself or delegates to people whom he knows to be skilled enough for the job in hand, yet how often do we leave somebody alone at the helm because everything seems to be going nice and smoothly?

With a small crew what else can we do? In my case, though, I made an entirely false assumption. I even felt a bit conscious that I was an amateur in the presence of a professional who would see as plainly as I could that the saltings were covered but that the channel lay to starboard and between the beacons. Nowadays I would have the horse sense and tact to look over his shoulder unobtrusively until quite satisfied that he knew his butt from his elbow.

The skipper carries the can and in a small cruiser it is very difficult to be a good skipper. A big-ship master or a trawler skipper or, for that matter, an offshore racing skipper all have one thing on their side that a cruiser skipper may not have. They have a clear purpose. They are either making a scheduled passage with cargo or passengers or catching fish or following a racing course, and no matter how nasty the conditions may get, nobody questions that the ship should be pushed on. In a cruiser, however, apart from making the passage from A to B there may seem no good reason why the crew should be subjected to unnecessary hardship. The cruiser skipper therefore may feel personally responsible for the discomfort of his crew and the crew may well ask why in hell they should be lumping into a force 6 at dusk when they could as well have waited for the weather to ease or headed for another and easier destination.

The temptation to put it to committee is strong. 'What do you think, then?' a skipper might ask of his retching and wretched crew.

'Shall we plug on for a bit or nip back into so-and-so? I don't mind either way – what do *you* want to do?' He loses out both ways. If they turn back and the wind shifts and eases they have wasted a day and if they keep going and it eases they congratulate themselves; if it stays nasty they blame him. 'We should have gone back,' they mutter. None of this relates to my fiasco but it is all part of the skipper role.

The big-ship master and the others are permitted the right of less clouded judgement too. Their first duty is the proper management of the ship and feelings and family relationships don't come into it, but in a typical family-crewed cruiser it is very different. To begin with, a great many women, wives, have been introduced to cruising willy-nilly and they have no real liking for it and there is no good reason why they should. They also know their husbands and they know when they are worried and bluffing – and the husbands *know* that they know. A wife may be scared out of her wits and being only human she takes it out on *him*. Now we have a skipper subjected to a two-way stretch and likely to make a silly and dangerous mistake for the sake of getting out of the nastiness and to justify his decision to sail in the first place.

I have never managed to be an ideal skipper despite a lifetime of skippering. My idea of the ideal skipper is somebody who is quietly decisive, who makes a decision but is flexible enough to diverge from it yet strong enough to stand by it, come what may, if it is the right one. Afterwards, whatever the outcome, he neither crows about it nor seeks to justify his actions and, apart from being very concerned about the comfort and pleasure of other people, he gets his priorities right. I have never met such a person.

An aspect of pilotage or eyeball navigation crops up in my sorry little tale – angles. We're concerned with charted land and seascape, direction to go and sense of direction without reference to the compass. When we originally turned to enter that creek there may have been a *feeling* of making a ninety-degree turn and proceeding straight ahead. Later, starting off from our anchorage, there could have been an instinctive feeling that the way out should therefore be another straight line and, in due course, another ninety-degree turn up the main channel. With nothing but a glittering expanse of water ahead and the beacons inconspicuously over to starboard, the Commander followed his nose.

It can happen again and again when retracing an earlier course. It happens in cities when we *feel* as if we have made a number of right-angle turns around the blocks and should arrive back in the main street when in fact the streets have been curving away and the corners have been bends and not right angles at all. Instinct alone is unreliable, while instinct aided by chart and compass is what conning a ship is all about.

How fast does a yacht sink? Well, obviously it does depend on the size of hole that is knocked in her, but there are plenty of holes and sinking yachts which have been abandoned sooner than they need have been and some that need never have been abandoned at all. Conversely, there are cases of crew vainly battling with an inrush when all attention should have been given to preparing to abandon and making distress signals.

Holing, like such other instant emergencies as fires and 'man overboard', produces crew shock. The sort of emergency that develops slowly, although perhaps in an equally deadly manner (and I have in mind lee shores in severe gales and the build-up towards a collision), gives a crew time to consider what to do in advance of the crisis. When a boat is holed by hitting an obstruction, for instance, the impact noise, the lurch and the sudden inrush of water can induce panic. The actual noise of the water is not necessarily an indication of how big the hole may be. On the other hand, the sound and feel of the impact (as in our case) may make it pretty clear that bad damage can be expected.

All hulls, other than the completely flat-bottomed box-like shapes, narrow and taper somewhat down to the bilges and so this restricted area fills very quickly and noisily. Water begins swishing up from under the cabin sole as the boat rolls and unless it is quite obvious where the damage has taken place it may be some minutes before a crew can find and evaluate the hole. In some cases, where a GRP boat has a complete inner moulding forming cabin sole, bunk sides, galley and so on, they may never be able to see it at all.

As the water level rises it appears to slow down once the narrow bilge has been filled. Also, if the actual hole is completely submerged, the sound of the water gurgling in is overlaid by the rushing and swirling caused by the motion of the boat. By then the cabin sole may be awash and to all appearances the boat will be gone within minutes. The odds are that unless the leak can be found and staunched she is certainly going to sink, but how soon is still in doubt. A really good hand bilge pump being worked at full capacity, say sixty to seventy strokes per minute, may be chucking out up to twenty-five gallons per minute, or a good deal less. A man with a bucket might bail out about the same, but even moderately serious damage may be allowing sixty to seventy gallons per minute of leakage.

It is dangerous to bandy figures, however. As an experiment I once took out my log impeller to leave a one-and-a-half-inch-diameter hole. Having emptied all stores from bottom lockers, I then stood by with a stopwatch intending to allow a five-minute interval; after half that time I chickened out and bunged up the hole. In two and a half minutes she had taken in forty gallons, measured when emptying her later. That was a very small hole, though, and my twenty-gallons-per-minute bilge pump could have coped with it. Real damage could hardly have caused a smaller hole. Had it been even twice that size, but inaccessible, with the boat at sea I would have been in a dangerous predicament without a second pair of hands.

It is not just a case of how much water a bilge pump worked by hand can shift and how much a bucket can bail as much as how long a crew can keep it up. Also, while two people are pumping and bailing like mad, who else is available for finding and stopping the leak, getting a distress call out, inflating a dinghy and packing a bag of essentials? Even having a liferaft only half-answers those questions.

Take two actual cases as examples. Obviously one was a big yacht since her exhaust pipe was of six inches diameter. When this came adrift, and because the exit could take in water, she sank within five minutes. The crew couldn't reach the leak, but by keeping their cool they had the dinghy inflated, a May-day call sent and a bag packed with food, water and essentials and they abandoned her in good order. In the other case the yacht hit a rock and slid off into deep water. Water was gushing in on either side of the stem from four separate holes which the crew couldn't manage to block. They too abandoned in good order but it took over ten minutes and the yacht sank fifteen or twenty minutes after being holed. What is interesting about both accounts is that, with a crew of three in the first and a crew of two in the second, there was no mention of trying to keep afloat by pumping and very little said about any attempt to stop the leaks. One may assume that in each case the damage was so obviously mortal that manpower was applied to the urgent need to abandon, and, as it turned out, quite correctly so.

It is very easy to theorize about plugging holes. The epic case must surely be that of Bill King, holed by shark or whale attack in the Roaring Forties and actually managing, singlehanded, to heel the yacht on the opposite tack in order to get at the damage in his bilge and nail a makeshift patch over it.

If you could get at the hole could a cushion or pillow be held down hard on it by wedging? With what ? Few modern yachts carry much in the way of either tools or bits of timber and to improvise takes time which you can't afford. With only two or three people aboard (one at least might be in a state of panic) should you invest time and precious manpower in trying to bung up the hole, pumping or preparing to abandon ship? It is a question which I hope never to have to answer, because there won't always be a handy stretch of beach to run her on.

A final thought on this sober subject. Once a hull becomes half-awash she loses stability, lolls around like a drunken man, and fore and aft trim alternates between bow and stern as unchecked water below surges to and fro. Anyone who has been in a dinghy which is awash to her seats will understand this. In anything of a sea, then, and with crew moving around on deck or below, her final plunge could be much more imminent than if the boat were lying quietly on a calm sea.

It has been shown again and again, though, that a crew should stay with the ship as their ultimate means of safety for as long as possible, albeit in the dinghy and with a knife ready in hand. Somebody has to make a very critical decision. No real hard-and-fast drill can be evolved other than having an emergency grab-bag containing food, water, flares, protective clothing, etc., always ready. The problem, I suppose, could be boiled down to: assess damage, decide whether to abandon. Both might have to be simultaneous. Dinghy or raft launching by one sensible crew member would never be a wasted measure, whatever the outcome.

3

A Run Ashore

I had anchored the schooner half a mile offshore with her nine feet of draught in a little under three fathoms at low water. The wind was south-west and offshore, our anchor was into good blue slipper clay and Jock and I were determined to have our run ashore. We were a charter ship and this particular charter party was an all-time bastard! Jock had come to me with a pair of muddy deck shoes which he'd found left by his bunk. 'Look,' he'd said, his rudimentary brow furrowed, 'fancy chucking them out. Why, they ain't bad wiv the mud off them.'

'Why, you stupid great ape, you're supposed to clean them,' I explained. He dropped them. Jock was my mate-engineer-deckhand and drinking partner. He'd come to me straight from a job in Southsea funfair, a 'diddy' in full drape, stovepipes, winkle-pickers and regulation duck's arse haircut. We had to have a run ashore.

We pulled ashore in the skiff, a light ten-footer with very little freeboard but easy to drag up the cable or more of soft mud foreshore – which also kept our charter party on board and at their bridge foursome. The Sloop in Wootton Bridge was a mile away up the lane and we clumped up in our boots, carrying the paddles and rowlocks. It was starting to rain, but the wind was no more than a gentle breeze.

It was a good evening and by chuck-out time Jock and I were well flushed, fully restored and even benign towards the bunch out on board. We strode off back down the lane at the brisk and purposefully fast clip common to near-drunks which is meant to convey sobriety and would do so, could one but stay out of the ditch. The tide was high, the dinghy was just as we'd left her and the breeze was now a tree-tossing force 5 spiced with splatters of rain. It was as black as the inside of a cow.

Distantly we could make out our riding light and the softer glow of saloon lamplight reflecting on the foreboom. Beyond them was the empty blackness of the Solent with the great glow of Portsmouth as a backdrop. We launched off, I rowing, Jock slumped in the stern with hands in lap. We had no lifejackets. In the early fifties one never had. I settled to a steady stroke, feeling the brisk wind astern and the wavelets growing from ripples to lippers, then wavelets to waves as distance increased. It was easy work. I raised my voice in song. I was awake, Jock was awake and I had a mission to wake any other son-of-a-bitch who had the temerity to be asleep. I wasn't drunk, though, and a corner of my mind was monitoring events. For instance, I was suddenly aware of a wave slopping in over the stern; so was Jock. 'Aw bloody 'ell!' he roared, outraged.

We both realized then that the dinghy was half-full and that, booted, we hadn't noticed the rising water level. The sluggish motion which had allowed the sea to board us was growing rapidly worse. What we did not realize then was that one of us had kicked out the cork which acted as bung. . . . Lacking a proper bailer, we both set to work with our caps, bailing with desperate speed while all the time the dinghy was sweeping downwind and seaward, past the anchored schooner, beyond to where the waves were humping black against the far city lights.

What happened that night, the transition from brown-ale bliss to fear, has stayed in my mind. Never have I snapped out of anything so fast. How long did I struggle at those oars, head to sea, winning a few feet, losing them in the next squall, sobbing for breath and drenched by the spray that burst over our bows? Later, in a final lunge to grab hold of the topsides, we half-filled the dinghy again and almost lost our tenuous hold.

They were still at their bridge when we slopped forward past the saloon skylight.

Conclusions

Obvious though they may seem, the mistakes we made are repeated again and again by others and drownings from yacht tenders at night are horrifyingly many.

Take the case of a crew returning aboard, tired and ready for bed. Everybody knows that two trips should be made of it, but the temptation to overload – 'We'll be very careful' – is overwhelming. It was not a case of overcrowding with us though it was over*clouding*, the overclouding of judgement induced by a few drinks. There was a fresh offshore breeze and I knew about *fetch* and that half a mile offshore there would be a sizeable sea, wind-blown and demanding second thoughts at least. Quite apart from the incident of the bung, which in itself could have been fatal had the boat taken a slightly heavier sea aboard, there was my failure to position the boat correctly upwind of the schooner.

A downwind approach under oars is initially easy, so easy that the rower cannot judge the weight of the real task ahead when the time comes to turn head to sea in going alongside. If one does a lot of open-sea dinghy work under oars this may not be so, but in these times of marina berths and outboard motors there must be thousands of people unaware of the trap.

Once far enough from the shelter of the land astern, the wise plan is to bring the boat round and take a few experimental strokes into wind and sea to gauge the situation before resuming the course. It also depends very much upon the number of people and the arrangement of rowing positions. An eight-foot boat (or, for that matter, a smaller one) should have rowing positions both amidships and in the bows, otherwise with two aboard, if the rower is forced to sit on the centre thwart, the boat will trim heavily aft which is a regular cause of swamping by the stern. In our case I was rowing from the bows which trimmed us correctly but restricted my power by limiting the leverage on the oars due to the narrower beam at that point. With three aboard I could have pulled on the centre thwart, but the extra weight would have defeated me in any case once head to sea.

The placing of a dinghy alongside in these conditions is a study in itself. The boat should be rounded up while still a couple of ship-lengths to windward so that angle and rate of drift can be gauged, holding the dinghy straight by an occasional stroke. It is a surprise to see how fast she does set down and the distance narrows rapidly. The best plan is usually to aim to drop alongside at a point just forward of the main shrouds, where the curve of the bow begins (Fig. 1). This will mean that for an instant she will be pinned against the topsides long enough to allow for the shipping of the inboard paddle and for a line to be put aboard. The further forward the dinghy painter can be secured, the better, because the dinghy can then be dropped aft and the extra scope of painter will allow her to ride more quietly.

The final seconds prior to contact are vital. If it is misjudged, the dinghy may fall athwart the plunging bows and anchor chain and be swamped, while placed too far aft, and there is only one chance to grab hold before the dinghy is carried astern; if there is also a tide to contend with, it is even more critical. Likewise the handling of the oars must be slick (Fig. 2). Ship the inboard one too soon and the dinghy hits the yacht bows-on and out of reach for the oarsman who may be sitting amidships, but shipped too late it prevents the dinghy from coming alongside at all. If the passing of the painter is muffed for any reason though, *do not let anyone try grabbing from the stern of the dinghy*. This may seem insultingly elementary but *somebody* will try it. Better to lay clear and drop astern then lug your guts out to get back again.

This in itself is yet another problem. How long can one person at the oars keep up a sustained flat-out effort? Sure as hell there is no hope of changing places to give him a breather. The time it takes to ship oars, change seats and resume rowing means perhaps twenty or thirty yards lost downwind. The best that can be done is for the passenger aft to place his hands over those of the rower and push the oars, but it is seldom effective. Neither can the dinghy be struggled up as far as the stern of the yacht and a grab made. To attempt it is dangerous and usually a failure. Keeping about two oar's lengths away, she must be pulled ahead at least as far as the shrouds before making a quick side sheer and shipping of oars (Fig. 3).

Inflatables under paddles are hopeless from the start, as all soon learn. Either one makes a pair of extra long ones and learns the crossed-hands rowing technique, or it is a job for a reliable outboard motor. There is still a hidden risk connected with arrival alongside. Head to wind and sea and with a weighty engine on the stern, all that stops an inflatable from flipping bow over stern is crew weight forward. In disembarking a crew of, say, three adults, the midships one should go first and then the bowman with the stern man simultaneously shifting his weight forward (or stern man while bow shifts aft a shade). Whatever the type of dinghy, once alongside she will leap and crash while water trapped between dinghy and ship pours into the dinghy solidly.

In our case, when we had finished bailing and we discovered that we were already being swept past the schooner, as I turned to head the seas it was very apparent that our small dinghy could not survive in the windy tide-swept waters of Spithead further offshore. My one great fear was of snapping an oar. Pulling at full strength in a seaway is totally different from rowing quietly down the river at an even stroke. You cannot maintain an even stroke. Oar strokes alternate between Herculean tugs with full body weight and the thrust of both thighs to short oar jabs taken as a wave crest hisses by. You pull into a trough, catch a short jab to straighten her, lay back full to hold her

Fig. 1 Approaching towards a yacht in a dinghy with a current (1), turn into it (2) and row, losing ground (3), until coming alongside (4) at the shrouds. Later (5) secure dinghy alongside further aft.

Fig. 2 Shipping the inboard oar, the rower then holds on to the rail of the anchored yacht. Do not try to grab from the stern of the dinghy.

as the crest rises and then lay back hard again in a power stroke as the wave back passes below you. You need a toe wedged under a thwart and the blades must dig deep, but be feathered on the back-swing as well if the wind is strong.

Running, there is the risk of swamping, especially over the stern and in the dark. The bows may also knife in and take water aboard, but it is the stern hidden by the backs of the passengers where the real threat lies whether running or pulling into a sea. That is why fore and aft trim is so absolutely vital.

Fig. 3 Working up against wind and tide, get level with the bows
and then crab across.

4

Fire

This collection of maritime mishaps could not possibly be complete without at least one account of fire afloat – and I say one because I have been involved in three. None disastrous; two of them ludicrous and the third potentially disastrous but part of another story told elsewhere. In each case, though, there were a number of common factors: choking smoke, rapidity of spread and panic, plus the fact that with a bit of forward thinking and ordinary care none need have happened.

This incident happened in *Hoshi* in the fifties when she was privately owned, running charters with me as the skipper and working out of Chichester. The party that chartered us for a week of gentle sailing consisted of elderly gentlemen – six altogether – and as one of them explained twinkling with great warmth and good will, 'We don't know anything about sailing and just want plenty of good fresh air, but no storms, please.' I agreed to cancel storms. Had they known what I had in store (see also the chapter entitled 'There's Always Luck'), they might have settled for a storm and gladly.

We dropped down harbour and, it being late afternoon and the tide wrong for crossing Chichester Bar, came to our anchor under the lee of East Head. I was very glad that we had, for by next morning it had come in wet and windy out of the south-west and more wind was forecast. It blew a steady force 6–7 with touches of gale for the next three days, after which we were able to go out and make a memorable cruise to Poole. *Hoshi* would have been well able to cope with the weather, but I had in mind that stricture about storms and my young mate Jock and I were happy enough to sit below and get on with splicing up some new ratlines. Jock was aged about sixteen at the time, powerfully built but tending to fall asleep if you allowed him to lean against anything and it was this tendency that was almost the downfall of us.

28

One of our old gentlemen, not to be done out of his fresh air, measured out how many times he would have to walk from the stern to the bow and back again to make one mile. I forget the staggering figure but I well recall the tramp of feet, six pairs of them in the end, that went on interminably overhead.

To provide an abundant supply of hot water for everybody to wash and shave in the mornings there was installed in the galley a big tank holding about five gallons, with its own spigot and underneath it a six-wicked paraffin heater. Once the heater had warmed up, the circle of wicks would be turned very low and they would then burn safely all night. The important thing was to light the wick circle, then wait about five minutes before turning it down – and if you did *not* turn it down it tended to flare up. One of Jock's jobs was to attend to this water heater. The layout below consisted of a big after cabin with a passage leading forward, having the generator and loo to port and the engine below the companionway staircase, flanked by a single cabin to starboard. Then came the main bulkhead and the full-width saloon with a single cabin leading off to port and the door to the galley opposite to starboard. Passsing through the galley, a sailcloth curtain divided off the four-berth foc'sle with its work-bench, lamp locker, folding table and us.

I turned in soon after supper, after having a sniff at the weather which was moderating, and the usual over the side. I dozed off at once. Jock, it seems, followed the same routine on deck and then lit the heater, but he decided to wait the statutory five minutes on his bunk – on his back. Being Jock, he went out as though he'd been sandbagged. I don't know why I woke up, but through sleepy eyes I gazed at the canvas curtain which had a comfortably warm yellow glow behind it. 'It's mummy with a candle coming to tuck me in,' my mind fantasized. Then a red patch materialized in the centre and in an instant there came a tongue of flame and the whole thing was ablaze.

Yelling I leapt from my pipecot, thumping Jock as I tore past him, and then pulled up to stare in horror through the remnants of the canvas and into the galley. The whole of one corner surrounding the heater was on fire, the years of white paint bubbling and flaming, while below it the heater had boiled over and the escaping paraffin was running downwards, burning fiercely. Jock, in vest and pants, was making a curious booming noise in my ear.

We had two big old soda-acid fire extinguishers, conical in shape and older than Satan, one in the galley and the other on the bulkhead at the foot of the stairs, both rusted to their brackets. 'On deck – get aft – the other extinguisher quick!' I screamed at Jock. The dividing door opened and an old head poked in. 'Shut it!' I shouted; it slammed shut in haste.

I knew about reducing draught and confining the fire, but the rest would depend upon destiny. I wrenched at the fire extinguisher with the strength of panic and recalled the simple operating instructions which were to '*strike knob sharply on floor and direct at seat of blaze*'. I banged the protruding knob down on the galley sole. The extinguisher bounced. A wooden floor was no match for an ancient, long-undisturbed knob of any calibre and I began a mad dance, banging and thumping the knob against every solid-looking fixture within reach while the flames spouted and spread.

When at last the extinguisher hissed and bubbled into action it was very effective and I hosed and squirted with growing confidence as steam and smoke began to replace flame. Then, suddenly, I had won but the extinguisher was still spraying manfully. The smoke and fumes filled every inch of both galley and foc'sle and I coughed and choked, eyes streaming and blind with tears as, still clutching my active appliance, I blundered towards the foot of the foc'sle ladder and the open hatch above it. It was at that instant that Jock arrived and stuck his head down the hatch. 'I've got it!' he proclaimed, with an uncanny sense of prophecy, as the jet from my extinguisher caught him full in the face.

When the smoke had cleared we tore up the floor boards to make sure that no trace of fire or heat remained. Some of the bulkhead was still charring and I was not happy until we were standing in a foul slurry of seawater, cinders and charred canvas. The actual damage was mainly cosmetic but it had been a near thing and why the heater didn't explode I will never know.

Conclusions

Most fires begin with carelessness or an oversight of some kind allied to equipment which may not be quite as safe as it should be. I have already described the fire in which I was involved (see Chapter 1), which was due to an unlagged dry exhaust pipe running through an after locker situated *underneath the petrol tank* and stuffed with lengths of dry old rope.

A third fire in a big ketch aboard which I was deckhand on another delivery began by the main propeller bearing running hot and igniting a scrap of oily waste left handy for a bit of drama. There were other near-fires, such as the bogey stove which had a bit of 'protective' asbestos on the bulkhead behind it allowing the woodwork to smoulder beneath it, and yet another exhaust pipe brew-up caused by similar reasons to the after-locker one.

Fires can happen through over-familiarity, too. A friend of mine has a fine big wooden cruiser which he has owned for years and which was built for him in the first place. He is very experienced indeed. One autumn he and his wife were laying up, and having had the mast lifted out and laid on deck, they motored back to the mooring there to sleep aboard ready for hauling out next day. They had oil lamps safely gimballed on the bulkhead, and also a standing lamp with its base held to the table top by rubber shock cord so that, when the cruiser was at anchor in quiet waters, it could be used as a reading light. They had been using it this way for years and it seemed to be stable as a lighthouse. My friend is a careful man, but this time he had forgotten something. His mooring was in a river used by big ships which passed at long intervals, making a bit of wash to which the sturdy cruiser would normally respond without too much fuss. This time, though, her mast was lying on deck.

They heard the ship go by as they sat reading. Then came the wash. Instead of the usual gentle corkscrewing, the cruiser suddenly went mad, jerking around with a great and totally unforeseen violence which shot the lamp straight off the table and on to a settee where it spilled oil and went up in a whoosh of flame. Cool reactions, the right extinguishers ready to hand, plus instant discovery of the fire saved the ship, but a lot of damage was done to her furnishings below.

A fire aboard is another panic-breeding emergency and it is hard to guess in advance how any particular crew will react to it. You can simulate fires for practice but, apart from giving useful instruction in using fire extinguishers, it is no training for a real emergency. Smoke and fumes, especially those caused by burning plastics of various kinds, are dense and often toxic. If the fire has a real hold, they also hide the source of the flames from the frantic crew who may then waste their fire extinguishers by triggering them off too soon. Extinguishers work by cutting off the air supply that feeds the flames and cooling the burning surfaces – they smother the fire. A fire blanket does the same job except that in a small boat it isn't always possible to spread a blanket over the blaze unless it is a simple frying-pan sort of fire.

Extinguishers are expensive to buy, they need regular servicing and are not much fun. Dry-powder types are effective but their contents are incredibly messy to clean up afterwards and this factor may cause people to hesitate in using them if there is a chance that the fire can be controlled by some other means. This is, perhaps, a foolish reaction but understandable by anyone who has ever seen a dry-powder extinguisher set off accidentally. BFC or BTM extinguishers are highly effective and they can usually be used in controlled spurts; in contact with flame, however, they give off toxic fumes which are dangerous in a confined space such as a closed cabin. This is the gamble you take: can you extinguish the fire before the fumes affect you? I suppose the answer is probably yes, provided the fire is in the usual place – the engine or galley and therefore under the open hatch.

Our old extinguisher was squirting plain albeit filthy water, and it is a wonder that the burning liquid paraffin wasn't carried and spread by it. Water as an extinguishant shouldn't be forgotten, because it is there in unlimited quantity, and unless there is burning liquid to deal with and provided the yacht isn't in a marina hooked up to the mains electricity, water allied to a desperate man with a bucket has a wonderfully cooling value.

One thing that I had quite forgotten in our fire was the gas bottle which was stowed just the other side of the forward bulkhead. I will never again forget my gas bottle.

5

There's Always Luck

I think bad luck is more often a case of the steady accumulation of minor idiocies catching up on you and good luck is attributable to having subconsciously done a few right things prior to the occasion. Anyway, we had been berthed at Poole Quay for the night and as a result of the collective torpor of a shipload of males first thing in the morning, we didn't get underway until the ebb had well and truly started. Drawing nine feet aft and not knowing the deep-water channels off Brownsea Island all that well, we should have stayed where we were.

It was a hazy, pearly morning with the lightest of following breezes as we went down harbour. I was motoring because otherwise the ebb would have robbed us of what little steerage way we had and *Hoshi* in a following ghoster handled like a piano on a barrow. We had our bows on the entrance off Sandbanks and Brownsea on our starboard beam when my mate Jock, who was honorary engineer as well, came up from below and rushed to look over the side. He turned upon me, a face of huge agitation opening and closing his mouth in an effort to form a message. It came at last. 'Pump's packed up!' he said, with his eyes popping, 'We've got to stop her before she seizes.'

It was not unknown for the cooling water pump to languish or for other shenanigans to occur, but it couldn't have chosen a worse place. We *had* to keep steerage way for another few cables so that I could get the schooner clear of the moored yachts and find a spot where we could anchor. 'Leave her be, for God's sake. I've got to keep her steering Jock,' I said with urgency. 'Give me another couple of minutes.'

'She'll seize solid any minute – I only just seen it.'

'Then she'll have to seize, mate!'

And thirty seconds later the engine gave a terrible cry and died. The silence was awful. I looked around me frantically, but there wasn't anywhere that I could let go the anchor without bringing up and scything round in a huge arc to side-swipe some innocent little yacht with our seventy-foot length. I felt my toes curl and my scalp crawl. I just daren't try it. The party of benevolent old gentlemen who had chartered this basket of jokes sat blinking happily in the sunshine, totally and enviably oblivious to our plight. I whistled a few bars of requiem mass, but my lips were dry and I made a poor hissing noise. I had to try *something*.

I fisted the wheel to starboard with the last of my steerage way. If I could bring her to the wind I might then sheer her across the tide *through* the moorings towards the island. She turned in slow motion as I called to Jock to get the sheets in and her bowsprit traced a lazy arc across the Brownsea shore. You've seen those dream sequences on TV with girls wearing yards of floating muslin who move with a misty slowness, but compared to our turn they are going like clockwork roosters.

There was one little cruiser with her owner sitting in his cockpit having a shave. Our bowsprit missed his shrouds and slid over his head – I remember the open mouth black against the shaving soap. The ebb was boiling out now and we sogged across it, making about forty-five degrees to the stream and setting down at a tremendous rate, missing mooring buoys and moored craft by inches, as I held her as tight on the wind as I could, consistent with having any control at all, while Jock bounded around setting anything that looked re-motely like a sail. The old gentlemen laid down their morning papers and watched this brisk exercise appreciatively.

At last there was only the line of big – really big – and very expensive yachts ahead and I knew why the old bitch had allowed me to dodge the smaller fry. There was a huge motor yacht lying ahead and downtide, purest white she was, nobody aboard it seemed, and thank Him for that at least, for it was plain what was afoot. She, like some of the other big yachts, was moored to a huge circular rubber-rimmed buoy shaped like a doughnut and at one time a flyingboat mooring.

The distance narrowed. The ebb was swirling past that buoy like the bastion of a bridge on the Rhone and I knew that I had left it too late to bear away and that there was no way in which I could luff to windward uptide of it; so I tried. I rammed the wheel hard up against the stops. 'Thousands . . .' I mourned, 'thousands of pounds' bloody damage . . .'

We hit the buoy. It made contact just forward of the beam with a

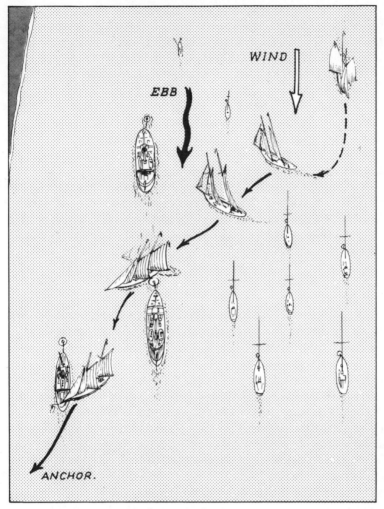

Hoshi among the moorings.

heavy jolt. For roughly half a lifetime we just hung there, pinned by the tide, but fifty tons of wood, iron and old men clutching newspapers in tight fists carries some way at even the slowest of sailing speeds and, awed, I watched the buoy begin to roll aft along our topsides, amidships and then – oh, the wonder of it – abaft our beam. Like a seesaw she inclined her bows downtide and the buoy, turning faster now, rumbled aft to emerge from under our counter with a rattle of chains like Marley's ghost.

35

Our bows windmilled downtide as, deprived of all steerage way, she drifted. Then the sails took a hand and I felt a tiny response from the helm. The bowsprit turned a scornful finger towards the gleaming topsides of another millionaire's joy and, as we swept past her stern, it picked off her varnished jackstaff like a gardener singling out the radishes.

'Oh God, let *go*!' I howled. Jock got there first, though, and yanked the cable stopper. The anchor was still at the stem, where it always was for leaving harbour, and away it went along with almost all the forty-five fathoms of stud-link until old dead spiders, fag-ends and toffee papers were erupting up through the naval pipe.

We brought up safely. I whimpered and fumbled for my pipe and tobacco. One of the old gentlemen tapped me on the shoulder. 'I would just like to say that that was truly remarkable seamanship,' he congratulated. Yes, it had been remarkable, and who was I to argue?

Conclusions

As the reader toils his way through these pages, a moral shines forth like a lighthouse and it is that unless you have an auxiliary engine that is reliable it is far wiser to behave as though you didn't have one at all. When it works it then becomes a bonus, but the real handling of the vessel must be under sail and all problems must be tackled as sailing ones. I know all this and yet like a wife with an unfaithful husband, or vice versa, I forgive and forget, keeping only a small mistrust alive until next time. In my own defence, I *did* act on this small mistrust by keeping my anchor ready to let go. My present boat is new and the diesel engine is new. It has once let me down, however, and although I trust it to take me through lifting bridges (the acid test) I never take the headsail off the forestay nor put the coat on the mainsail, neither do I motor close uptide or to windward of obstructions if I can avoid it and my anchor is always ready for use.

My first error was to put almost total trust in an engine that I knew to be temperamental. We should have left earlier on the last of the flood which would have meant having a light wind against a weak tide and it would then have been far easier to manoeuvre, to turn her into the wind which would have been a stronger *apparent* wind. Alternatively I could have waited for the last of the ebb and had the extra option of deliberately running her aground if all else failed. That would have *stopped* her and with the small range of tide in

Poole which would have almost finished ebbing she would only have been stuck for a short while. As it was, I left with a nice fast ebb under us which reduced what might have been a three-knot following breeze to almost an apparent calm.

Turning *Hoshi* into the wind meant that although she was still moving downtide over the ground, closehauling her increased the apparent wind just marginally enough to give me some helm; the rest was luck. I might, of course, have let go the anchor on a short scope in the thick of the moorings. She would have brought up, swung half-head to current and either clobbered some moored yacht half-heartedly or dragged slowly back on to another, in which case we could have fended off and then paid out scope to bring us up. But it is equally possible that we might have fouled a mooring on the bottom and compounded the mess.

The effect of apparent wind is familiar to everybody who sails, but it has two different aspects. A moving boat transforms a true wind, altering its speed and angle according to the boat speed and point of sailing, while the other aspect is the *tide wind*. Here we have a boat in a total calm at dead slack water and as the flood or ebb begins and increases in rate, the sails find their own wind according to the speed of the current. This means that on a two-knot current over the ground she has a two-knot current of air pressing her sails. It also means that she has a limited control athwart the airstream, but it might just be enough.

The ease with which navigation buoys can be hit is another feature of apparent wind in light airs. Given a tide under you and a following wind such as we had, the fact that the rate of tide is gradually increasing as the channel narrows may not be realized right away. The breeze seems to die a little but the bows are aimed clear of the buoy ahead, which may be still well distant and no cause for immediate concern. Before you know it, the buoy is only a few lengths dead ahead and the helmsman, who may not be very experienced, only uses a few degrees of helm, then realizes too late that the yacht is barely answering. Also, tidal currents don't always set straight down the channel but sometimes slightly athwart it, perhaps as a result of the eddy setting out of a bay or around a small headland.

There is a further point worth considering about colliding with a moored or anchored yacht. On one occasion we were lying at anchor in a Brittany river, slightly athwart the ebb. A small yacht was coming downstream under main and a big genoa which probably masked the helmsman's view because he certainly didn't see us until too late. He then had an equal choice of luffing, which would certainly have meant a glancing collision with our port bow, or of bearing away on full rudder and gybing round. He chose the latter. Two things happened. He picked up speed instead of losing it as he would have done by luffing and misjudgement meant a square-on collision instead of a glancing one. His stem iron punched straight through our topsides.

In a modern short-keeled hull you can spin around in a very tight turn either by luffing or bearing away, but if you do either it must be with gusto – helm full over in one steady sweep and mainsheet freed if bearing away. We are told that the helm never needs to be put *full* over, but provided it is not slammed over faster than she can answer it – which slows a boat – it is far more positive than a tentative little jab. It is when we manoeuvre half-heartedly, in uncertainty, that things tend to get hit. It is far less expensive to hit a glancing blow by tacking than to hit the target in the course of a gybe. Furthermore, when luffing the sheets can be freed if collision becomes inevitable, but there isn't a damned thing we can do to slow her in mid-gybe.

6

On the Beach

This time I wasn't the skipper, I was the mate and therefore not the one who took the decisions, which makes telling the tale a good deal easier. It happened during my early days in dear old *Hoshi* and she had the same dear old engine that was to be my private nightmare for years to come.

The owner was 'Chunky' Duff, dead these many years and, despite the impression created by this episode, a brilliant seaman. As a skipper he was my personal idol, for he was cool in trouble and a fine ship handler of great experience. We had an early-season charter party aboard and we left the lock a Deauville on high water to motor seaward into a fresh dead noser out through the deep-water channel, which was flanked by a training wall on one side and shallow sands on the other. It was narrow, too narrow for us to beat or even to motorsail, so it was engine or nothing for about half a mile. The lock gates closed behind us and they wouldn't be opening again that tide.

Our ageing, snuffling auxiliary inched us over the ground at a crawl while we pitched and corkscrewed into the short sea. Chunky was on the wheel, humming the way he did when none too happy, and I stood nearby holding on and none too happy either, for we both knew what would happen if that engine should stop. Neither of us voiced our thoughts. The bows were rising to the seas with hardly a spatter of spray and falling into the troughs where we'd lie stationary with foam seething alongside. Then *Hoshi* would hoist herself painfully forward to meet the next crest, only to lie, all way lost, in the trough again. 'Teee, tum tee,' Chunky moaned. *Hoshi* inched forward again, heavy as a sack of Bibles.

'We might as well get the mainsail on her,' drawled Chunky. I knew that drawl. I rallied some help and got the main on her and predictably it flogged and thundered, jangling its chain nips like a carthorse on the trot. It also slowed us even more, but Chunky drew strength from having that mountain of mildew wagging about over his head. We had almost reached open water when the great silence came. 'God, it's stopped!' everybody howled in unison. 'It's bloody stopped,' said Chunky, making it official. God received the news unmoved. The new silence was broken only by the racket of the mainsail and the anticipatory lip-smacking of the seas under our counter.

'Foresail, please, jib and staysail', Chunky said quietly, as if ordering fancy cakes. He gave her port wheel to fill the mainsail. 'Hum, hum, humpity hum,' he sang anxiously. Falling over each other, we got the rest of the sail on her and she began to shoulder her way over the seas on starboard tack, out of the deep channel and into hazard. I got the lead and took a swing. We drew nine feet and in the trough I had a bare two fathoms. The skipper received this information with a nod and brought us harder on the wind while we sharpened in the sheets all round. Our gaff foresail set like baggy trousers and the jib like a roadman's tent, a hen in a high wind had a better aerofoil shape and predictably we lost way. We were heaving and heeling, making all the right sound effects, but we were like the pirate ship in pantomime jerking around yet getting nowhere. Humming like a beehive, Chunky freed her a bit. 'We'll put her about,' he said.

She gathered a bit of way and he put the wheel up, her bows came round hesitantly, came head to wind and up forward. I had the jib and staysail aback, waiting. Nowadays owners of modern boats rarely know what it is to hang in stays, but the big yachts like *Hoshi* don't spin on their heels; they have to be sailed round in a wide sweep and you rely upon their massive weight and impetus to get through the wind. We had the weight, but that short sea beat us and we began to fall astern. Chunky backed his helm and she paid off on starboard tack again.

It was like sailing in glue. Even freeing her off made little difference and with the knowledge of the shallows below us we waited, soles of feet tingling. We tried it again but with the same result: she fell back wearily on to starboard tack. Down below somebody was still trying to re-start the engine and the 'wow, wow, wowww' of a tiring battery told its own tale. Could we bear away and gybe her round? This alternative was not acceptable because we all knew that it would mean heading further inshore and the water was too shoal for that.

The dream slowness of our pace was like one of those nightmares in which you try to run but find that your feet are too heavy to lift and by then I knew the cause. When a vessel moves in water which is barely deep enough to float her she 'smells the seabed', as the saying goes – her motion creates a heavy drag. I was thus lost in the realms of science when she hit and the shock was thereby all the greater.

There is no sensation like it. There is a deep, heavy jolt and you sag at your knees. We all called loudly upon the Lord in ragged chorus and stood helplessly staring at each other as the old ship recovered and lurched forward only to hit again still harder, her tall masts whipping and from somewhere in the galley the rattle of a pan leaving its hook. She heeled to a puff and gamely got to her feet only to come down with a bang that snapped our necks forward. After that she moved forward no more but lay rising and slamming down, lurching to leeward, shoreward, with every crash. Then even her progress to leeward stopped and she just lay there and hammered while the seas broke solidly against her bilge as she heeled landwards.

Chunky ordered the sails off her and that was all we could do except wait. At first she took the blows on the solidity of her heel, then as the ebb quickened she put her bows down until she lay on the long flat of her keel, well heeled to port and lurching hard down. We waited in dread. At last we felt the first sickening crash as her bilge met hard sand and we lay at an impossible angle, all hanging on. Landing on her bilge was as dangerous as an athlete landing on one hip and I felt the pain as if it were my own body. Everything below was slipping and crashing, but now the seas were growing smaller

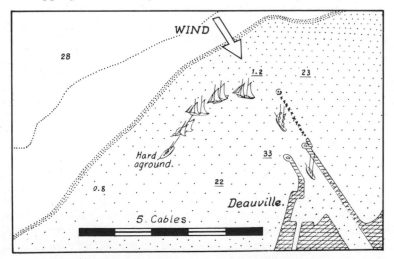

Deauville approach and entrance.

and by degrees the punishment decreased until we lay still as the water finally left us.

Then came the seaside holiday makers. First, an old man in a beret riding a bike: Gauloise stuck to his lower lip, he nodded *bonjour* as he passed under our bowsprit. Next was an assortment of bathers all sun-tan and belly button, chin-fringed young men and muscular matrons in swimsuits frilled at the hip – a disguise for their vast bottoms that gave the effect of delicatessen hams. Last came the horse and cart. It drove right round us with the driver pointing out features of particular interest to his passengers who nodded, well pleased with such an unusual seaside distraction. Meanwhile, our party perched wooden-faced in the best of British tradition, implying that all was normal and intentional, while Chunky and some more of us were rooting around under the bilge looking for any signs of external damage. A gingerish dog with an air of hurried importance cocked its leg on our rudder blade and three-legged it for the shore.

The situation was even worse than I have hinted. The tides were cutting and would continue to peak lower each day for another three of four days until they began springing again. In all, it would probably be a full week before *Hoshi* would fully float once more and although the weather was relatively settled the risk of a sudden deterioration was great. Within the hour our charter guests had packed and left, bound home via the ferry, and Chunky and I were left alone.

He reached the local Lloyds agent fairly easily via the phone, but it was some hours before I saw the two of them returning over the sands and the new flood was already well advanced. The agent did a good deal of head wagging, sighing and teeth sucking. If we couldn't get ourselves off on the flood during the coming night, we would become a valid insurance job requiring outside help. The agent hastened back to his office to report to London and take further advice; meanwhile, the night closed in on us and the breeze mercifully fell calm.

The angle at which we lay made it impossible to do any cooking aboard and one could only move around by walking on the side panelling, so, being very hungry by then, we waited until the flood tide came sneaking back and the hull was starting to lift before we tried to cook anything. Chunky was very hard up and the whole charter plan was simply to make *Hoshi* pay for her keep. He had bought her after the war – a pipedream come true, but even in those days a costly one. His pocket certainly didn't run to eating ashore while we still had food aboard. There was another reason for staying aboard: our dinghies were too heavy to drag all that way over the sand up the beach for the return trip and when the tide was out *Hoshi* was too vulnerable to thieves to be left. One of us had to be aboard.

There was a swell running still, despite the calm night, and with oil lamps swinging madly, the keel thudding heavily at intervals and the ship rolling, it was an uneasy meal we shared and uneasy too were the watches we kept until at last the ebb left her again and the world became sane and silent. We dozed until dawn, wedged uncomfortably in our pipecot bunks.

We had laid a heavy kedge out to seaward early in the game but the massive two-hundred-pound Nicholson main anchors were beyond our strength to shift, let alone dragging stud-link chain after them. Other plans were afoot, however. The agent came out to us. London was not going to take the risk of leaving us stranded on an open shore for another five or six days and a big tug, a sea-going vessel, had been chartered from Le Havre a few miles up the coast. The tugmaster would be arriving to survey the scene the next day. With amazing good luck, the weather remained settled and calm all that day and for a further night, then soon after low water the tug arrived and anchored off.

The tugmaster and his working party were as hearty a bunch of French cut-throats as I'd ever seen. They looked at *Hoshi* as she lay on her ear. 'Ai, ai, aiee!' they exclaimed in dismay. 'Ah la-la, what theeng theese, eh?' We weren't sure what thing and said so.

They hurled themselves into action. They had brought ashore a mass of gear, heavy ropes, blocks, shovels and much hessian padding, also various canvas bags which they now opened. A picnic was spread on the sand while Chunky and I stood awed by the long flutes of French bread, cheese, pâté, cold sausages and a regiment of wine bottles which were quickly and expertly opened. Getting the message, Chunky climbed back on board for more wine left behind by our charter party, and more bread, tinned sardines and pineapple chunks. The party went on until every bottle was empty – an uproarious bunch of villains bellowing and singing with bulging mouths, jabbing pineapple chunks on the points of huge sheath knives and offering them to us all in the greatest of high spirits. We wondered when the hell they would get down to the matter in hand.

At last they had finished and the last moustache was wiped on the final sleeve. '*Alors!*' the tugmaster cried, issuing a stream of commands, and like a troupe of acrobats cartwheeling into the ring the gang went into action. A massive coir cable was taken right round the schooner hung off at intervals from the deck so that it girdled her just below the washports, all heavily padded with hessian and making it plain that our bitts were not to be trusted. Then a keel channel a foot and a half deep and about four feet wide was dug straight out over the sand for perhaps fifty yards to a point at which the tugmaster deemed the ship would be able to float properly. Along this, from our stern and running well out into the water, was laid the towing hawser buoyed for later recovery at its outer end. The working party, with much handshaking, retired back aboard the tug and the waiting began.

It was a high tide that day about 6.00 p.m. A boat brought the tugmaster back and then returned, leaving him aboard with us. *Hoshi* was upright, or nearly so, and still hard aground, the tides having cut considerably since our original grounding. We could feel and hear the scrunching of sand echoing up through the hull; fortunately the swell was only slight by that time but perhaps a little more of it would have helped. It was almost high water. The tugmaster walked up and down, sizing matters up and not much liking what he found to judge by the sighs and eye rolling. Then he raised one arm and placed a whistle somewhere under his moustache.

I have mentioned that the towing hawser was secured to our *stern*, this being necessary because our stern was lying to seawards of our bows. Had it been secured to the bow, the tow would have meant dragging the ship round through about one hundred degrees of a circle before we were in line for towing. I have also referred to the tug being ocean-going and this was no overstatement since Le Havre was a base for big salvage tugs and this one was the smallest available at the time. The tugmaster blew his whistle and made delicate movements with his arm. There was a blossoming of white water under the stern of the tug and the towing hawser began to rise from the water – a sort of shudder ran through the old schooner as the girdle around her hull began to stretch and creak and tremble. We stood well back, gritting our teeth. The tugmaster lowered his arm and the hawser sagged slack again.

Some conversation took place in French which I couldn't follow and, what with Chunky jerking his eyebrows up and down, the tugmaster spreading his hands and lolling his head around and both of them blowing their cheeks out, it was like a music-hall double act. Plainly a state of *impasse* had been reached, because Chunky spread *his* hands and the tugmaster made an OK-don't-blame-me gesture. He raised his arm once more and blew the whistle.

This time the towing hawser came taut more quickly and went on growing taut until it stretched from tug to schooner in a humming catenary and *Hoshi*, shuddering more violently, suddenly lurched upright, paused, then gave one gut-wrenching leap stern-first seawards. She lurched again. This time her rudder blade bit into the sand and suddenly, with a snapping of bolts, the whole worm steering gear rose from its bed and the spoked wheel swung upright like a teak and brass daisy. In a series of sickening jolts and lurches we were dragged bodily seawards until, reaching deeper water, the torture ended and we floated freely. The whistle blew, the arms waved and the hawser fell slack.

We were towed to Le Havre lashed alongside the tug because we had no means of steering. It was a short trip and an anxious one, far too fast for peace of mind as we see-sawed and jerked against a mound of fat fenders, but we arrived and were berthed at last and left once more to our own devices. We were to lie in the hands of a local yard for over two weeks while the hull was surveyed, the steering gear was repaired and the engine declared trouble-free yet again by an engineer of great optimism and little prudence.

At that time it was not only very difficult to obtain foreign currency above about a £10 tourist limit but Chunky didn't have much anyway. Meanwhile, however, we had to eat. We finished the provisions aboard, ending up with curious meals using up charter delicacies such as tinned tongue and shrimps with Oxo cubes. Then, realizing that there was a market for empty wine bottles in France, we set forth, carrying sacks of empties, to do the rounds of all the *estaminets* within walking distance. There may have been a national shortage but it didn't extend to Le Havre and we finally dumped the lot on a bomb site.

Some insurance money came through just as we were beginning to consider the back door of the Little Sisters of the Poor. The cost of hiring extra crew or paying ferry fares from England was not to be considered. It was time we were gone before the weather broke if we were to get home in time for our next charter.

The weather was very properly dead on our nose and fresh. It took us ninety hours of beating watch and watch under plain sail and falling asleep at the wheel. When at last we made our final board and Chunky said 'I think we can ease sheets a bit now,' we were both completely exhausted.

Conclusions

Engines, when they are old and ailing, are very like human beings. First the varicose veins need to be fixed, then there is a rheumatic knee, and that is treated only for some other organ or joint to start failing. With engines, though, the fact that an actual fault has been diagnosed by the engineers and replaced or fixed tends to give us wary optimism. Only when they can't isolate any one fault and yet the engine seems to behave itself after being tinkered with do we regard it with a cold and canny eye. Prior to that cruise our old petrol Gray had been thoroughly overhauled and it had run like a bird until we really needed it. That same engine and others of similar erratic behaviour were the catalyst in the majority of my misadventures related in this book and the background story is always the same: the engineers have found a fault and fixed it, *ergo* there exists a state of semi-trust until the next time.

There are times when an operation has the mockers on it from the word go. In our bones we know it and yet we carry on, alert but hoping, subconsciously knowing that we should be doing the sensible thing with all its complications and inconveniences and staying safely in harbour until the wind shifts or some other factor makes it safe to go. I think many of us get into trouble because we are trying to impose time schedules on our sailing, to get back in time for work or, as in our case, because the charter time was up.

We could have anchored right there in the channel. There was the risk of being side-set by the tidal current but it was the lesser risk. When we began trying to sail our way out over the shallows and the keel 'smelled the bottom', we both felt it from the ship's behaviour. With hindsight we should have anchored *then* even though, at the end of a suitable scope, her heel might have been thumping the sand, but the urge to keep trying is too strong and – who knows? – there just might have been a deeper patch that would have allowed us to get free. Some years later, in St Peter Port, I tried to sail out of the harbour anchorage for the fun of it. I had a clear tack to port, giving just sufficient room to open the entrance enough for a long starboard tack out. We broke out the anchor and paid her off to port smartly enough, but I had forgotten how shallow it was and I had forgotten about 'smelling the seabed' until the helm went dead in my hands as, with the sails full and pulling mightily, she laboured over the ground. I knew that she would miss stays and fall off among the anchored boats. The kedge and its warp were still on deck from earlier use and I gambled on something I had read. Quickly my mate led the warp forward outside all to windward and when he was ready I ordered the kedge away and began my tack, snubbing on the kedge to snatch her bows round then casting it off completely. It did the trick but it cost us half a day grappling for the kedge while *Hoshi* lay at anchor outside the harbour.

The situation in which a vessel bumps bottom, goes on, bumps again and so on is the origin of the expression 'touch and go' and although the vessel may win clear under engine or with the wind free, it is very unlikely that she can get away with it under sail alone and hard on the wind. Once she stops and gets her heel stuck she – and almost any sailing vessel, I dare say – will pay her bows off downwind and stick solid as she comes upright. Again with hindsight, we should have anchored when that moment came, because even if it would not have prevented her bumping further to leeward harder and harder aground, we would have been laying out cable to windward as we did so.

We might then have got off by our own efforts on the following tide since as it happened the night was so calm. We might have heeled her to decrease her draught by laying one of our two ten-foot dinghies alongside, rigging a strop fore and aft and under the bottom and filling her with water. By booming her away from our topsides and with the powerful throat halyard attached to the midship point of the strop, we just might have heeled her enough to be hauled off on her own anchor windlass. It might also have been a total waste of time, but only our labour would have been lost and I have heeled down small yachts in this way. In any case, we would have been lying with our bows to seaward and if the tug had been needed, her job would have been done more easily and maybe without rudder damage.

The tug was engaged to do a job and the price was agreed and paid by our insurance company which preferred the bill for that to the risk of total loss by leaving us on the beach. The rigging of the towing girdle was very interesting. I think the experts would have done this even if the tow off had been bows first because yacht bollards, heavy as ours were by modern standards, are just not up to that sort of emergency strain and lifeboatmen faced with yacht rescue and towage have enormous problems to overcome. Modern yacht stem fittings, bow fairleads, are usually too small to contain a towing warp; also, the cheeks of the fairlead, being of stainless steel plate rather than well-rounded castings, are too sharp. Neither do many yachts have a foredeck bitt or cleat fixed strongly enough to take the snatching of a tow in a seaway without tearing out and possibly opening up the deck as well. In a small yacht, in bad weather, it is impractical to think about rigging a girdle around the hull, but perhaps around the coachroof and cockpit coamings? The big problem would be to keep it from slipping up and trapping the helmsman during the tow – plus the time it would take to rig.

7

Pure Thoughts
and Cold Showers

The Outward Bound Sea School's ketch *Warspite* was a powerful ninety-tonner, the ex-yacht *Bluebird* once owned by Singer the sewing-machine king. She was run and officered by the Alfred Holt Shipping Company, the original founders of the school during the Second World War and summer and winter she cruised between Aberdovey and Abersoch Bay across perhaps twenty miles of the wide, shallow Cardigan Bay. Her crew would consist of fourteen lads plus skipper, mate, engineer and a watch officer accompanying each batch of boys. Courses at the OBSS were of one month's duration and perhaps four watches of boys would be taken to sea in turn.

I was a watch officer and the only member of the nautical staff not on loan from Alfred Holt or the Anglo-Saxon Oil Company, which also supplied officers. It was ironic that, as a mere yachtsman, I was often the only officer with any real small-boat experience, the professionals being big-ship men on detachment for varying periods. In the summer it was one long albeit exhausting holiday and in the Welsh winter it was murder. The aim of the thing was self-discovery for young lads. The method was challenge, which began with cold showers and continued through every sort of strenuous activity likely to jerk the dazed and lack-lustre teenager into discovering his own potential. 'To strive and not to yield' was the motto. I once caught a lad having a quick smoke behind the boatshed. 'I'm fed up of striving,' he told me, 'so now I'm yieldin'.'

It was early February and bitterly cold. We had a new skipper on loan, a dour monosyllabic master mariner who had been brought up in Tasmanian ketches and who, for once, really sailed us. We left the quay at Aberdovey under sail, our engineer sulking in his tiny engineroom, and we cracked on to Abersoch with every stitch we could muster instead of the usual dull motorsailing passage under

49

main and mizzen. We anchored for the night under St Tudwals Island.

This was routine. We didn't expect to teach the lads how to sail, for which most of them were profoundly grateful, but with luck we could make them sick, cold and frightened, all of which was thought beneficial to the developing *id*. This time fourteen *ids* were in for a treat. By dusk we had shifted anchorage three times in seeking a lee from the island in a shifting wind and the wind was beginning to squall. It went into the south-east and began to blow great guns. In the ordinary way we would have laid at full scope with the engine running and rolled our guts out all night, but not with this skipper.

He stood for a long while in the doorway of the companionway deckhouse, snuffling like an old hound and mumbling to himself. He had on his carpet slippers and an ancient woollen cardigan and he looked like a sleazy old institute caretaker. The mate was my chum Stubby, a Merchant Service officer with a passion for sail. 'Mate,' called the skipper, 'double reef main and mizzen, small jib on the bowsprit, halfway in.' He snuffled some more and looked around, mumbling, then he turned and went below to the roaring warmth of the saloon bogey stove. It was almost dark by then. We roused out some of the brighter lads and set about reefing, a job that took us a full hour or more of dragging with frozen fingers at the board-like wet cotton sails. The main boom was, of course, chin high and the task of muzzling the flogging canvas in the dark was a bastard.

It was almost another hour before we were under way. The ketch had a big old handspike windlass with a gypsy that didn't quite fit the chain; there was a lot of it out. Tramp, tramp, tramp, then stagger as the chain slipped, jumping the gypsy, foot by foot, curse by curse. Gone were the clean thoughts and words. We blasphemed roundly, lads and officers alike. Then up main and mizzen and up jib and aback as the cable came slack. We fished and catted the massive Nicholson as the old ketch plunged clear of the semi-shelter and hit the full force of the Irish Sea gale.

The skipper – the Old Man – found a seat in the deckhouse from where he could watch and order the proceedings. He was no yachtsman to go plunging around in the cold and wet, heaving and humping about; he was the master and he cherished his right to keep his carpet slippers on. We had a lad on the wheel with a course to steer and we were getting the hell out of it, away from the killer land and out into open water. It was going to be a long, bad night. In fact it was going to be two long bad nights with a miserable day in between.

The lads on that cruise were a mixture of scrubbed-looking Conway Cadets, Borstal boys, public schoolboys, future galley boys, lads on probation and lads sent by industry as a 'reward' and in order to get a keen and searching character report at the end of it all. Once we were clear of the land, the seas were huge roaring monsters into and over which we laboured full-and-bye, hove hard down and swept by endless blasts of freezing spray. The night seemed eternal.

With dawn we were well out in St George's Channel and there we laid her to under backed jib and with the wheel lashed a'lee. The relief was awesome. By then all but one or two of the boys were helplessly and fruitfully seasick, but the Old Man insisted upon all doing a spell of lookout while Stubby and I did watch-and-watch. The Old Man kept the stove going and the engineer stayed in his pit, still bitterly offended. The motion was a soaring, twisting gyration, but robbed of the hammer and bang of closehauled sailing. Little spray came aboard but the deep wuthering moan from aloft as we heeled down and back seemed to penetrate our minds and bodies, leaving us constantly alert for some new sound presaging trouble. The day passed. Towards teatime the wind rose to what must have been force 9 or more and the Old Man ordered the storm jib on her.

Stubby and I did the job. For some reason which I now forget we had to go out on the bowsprit and it was snowing by then. I watched Stubby, who was outboard of me, suddenly disappear into a wave crest and emerge whooping and yelling. 'Christ!' he yelled exultantly, 'I . . . went to sea . . . for this and find it *here!*'

It was suddenly night again. The lads were now doing wheel watches because the ketch could no longer be guaranteed to hold her sheer hove-to and at intervals she would come up all shaking or pay off into the trough. The lads had to watch the compass heading ready to yell for assistance, although once we had begun these watches that old bitch behaved herself. The snow became a blizzard. The lads were supposed to be doing half an hour each, relieving each other automatically.

One of the boys had been the despair of the shore staff throughout the course with his stealing, swearing and lazy insolence. He had smoked, dodged and lied and he had continued to do so aboard the ketch. Stubby and I had kept no check on these watches, beyond ensuring that there was always a muffled form sitting braced behind the wheel all the time as the hours crawled by. He and I were doing two on and two off. There was no visibility at all on deck, only a ceaseless shriek of wind and the horizontal pummelling of snow

51

against one's back. The Old Man was still in his slippers, though, unsleeping and alert, the object of our black hate by virtue of his dryness and access to the stove. He beckoned me into the deckhouse during one of my tricks. 'Would you like something to warm you up?' he whispered. Visualizing a quick nip of scotch, I nodded my eager assent. 'Take one o' these, then,' he said, offering me a bag of striped peppermints.

I suppose it must have been shortly before dawn that we realized. We had known that the Conway boys to a man were very seasick, as had been the rest of that watch, but we hadn't known what was happening about the wheel watch itself – who was doing it. Lie, cheat and steal as he might when ashore, that scrawny little runt had taken over every watch from about midnight until we discovered the truth, taking him gently below, plying him with warmth and respect and awe. 'Someone had to do it. They're piss-poor them lot, so I done it!' he told us. Later, back ashore again, he was to revert to his evil little ways, but we knew and now he knew something preciously rare about living.

Had we but known it, there was a great hue and cry out for us. We had no radio (at that time the Post Office forbade even this ketch from using ship-to-shore communications) and we had virtually disappeared, feared lost. The Old Man, I believe, had a lot to answer for to shore authorities, but nothing to answer for as far as his instincts as a seaman went. With daylight the worst of the strength of the wind was going. We drew sheets and laid a course for home, reaching the offlying waters of the Dovey Estuary in the late afternoon and moving under sail and power to get in before dusk. There was one further problem with one further solution rooted in fine and traditional seamanship.

The bar at Aberdovey is notorious. Although it was a weather shore in that wind, a big swell was now running and in the hazy visibility we could see the line of breaking crests ahead marking the shallow bar itself. There was the only alternative of turning and running back to the uncertain Abersoch anchorage – or heaving to offshore again. The Old Man took the wheel and we stowed sail.

With the leadline going we sounded our way closer and closer, then began motoring up and down parallel to the line of breakers while the Old Man studied the run, size and moment of break. We must have been at it for twenty minutes, then he spoke. 'Get all the cans with lids you can find and fill 'em so they'll just float with that heavy oil *he's* got in the engine room – and bring the drum on deck.'

There must have been a dozen tins. We filled them and jabbed holes in each, then we motored back and forth while 'the best cricketers' lobbed cans towards the bar. Then we hauled off and laid a parallel slick. We waited some more. At length the Old Man seemed satisfied. We went in.

Did the oil truly take the menace out of the breakers? I really don't know; I only know that no water came aboard and the ketch ran in and over with no trouble at all.

Conclusions

Lest the final incident in this narrative and this particular solution to a dangerous problem should leave the reader with the impression that this is how the crossing of a breaking bar should be tackled, let me stress that this is *just not so*.

If a bar is breaking it is dangerous and not to be crossed except by local experts. Oil might well have stopped or helped to stop wave crests from forming and breaking but the size, steepness and length of waves would not have been altered and a small vessel could as easily have been broached and rolled as if oil had not been used at all. Our master mariner was a very competent and wise seaman who knew all about surf and as we motored up and down (in itself a lesson) he must have weighed up the character of the seas on the bar relative to the probable behaviour of the ketch. The story is interesting but best forgotten as an illustration of bar-crossing technique. The real lesson is the old one about the threat posed by the land in bad weather. Our master knew that his anchorage was tenuous and that he had a weak crew, he knew that he had a safe enough escape towards deep and open water and he knew that he had a powerful boat in excellent condition. He plainly also knew all about weathering winter gales in ketches – the Tasman Sea is notorious. If a small craft is safe and secure in a completely sheltered anchorage it is a very different matter and the worst that can happen is to drag ashore. As another tale in this book reveals, not all seemingly sheltered anchorages are safe ones, but safer nonetheless to human life than hanging precariously in the lee of a small island in a shifting gale.

Our skipper's apparent selfishness is something else. Was he truly dodging the misery of the open deck or was he conserving his own strength, the better to make sound decisions while his young, fit watch officers handled the ship? I think the latter was true. It sets a dangerous precedent among yachtsmen perhaps, but he was a real professional and hard as flint. He also made all the right decisions.

The young lad who showed such amazing fortitude and generosity, for whatever reason *he* gave, just brings home once again the truth that you never know whom you have aboard until the going gets really tough. I have often wondered what became of him and where and what he is now – a man in middle age.

Our ketch was a big vessel by modern yacht standards and in winter, in that sort of weather, she was pressed very hard. Had we been in a modern thirty-footer, I would not like to guess how we might have come out of it. A winter gale with bitterly cold wind has a far greater *pressing* effect upon sails than a warm summer gale of the same speed in knots or mph. This is a fact. Thames sailing-barge sailormen knew this. 'It's a *heavier* wind in winter,' they would tell you. Yachtsmen don't often make offshore winter passages in bad weather, but more and more owners keep their boats in commission longer each year and consequently the likelihood of meeting bad and *cold* weather increases. Not only are winds heavier but human tolerance is far, far less. And nights are a good deal longer too.

The ill-fated *Nicolette* which lost her mast on delivery passage following a skimped fit-out. Many years later she was to be run down by a French fishing boat in North Biscay, with tragic loss of life. *Chapter 1*. Photo: Roy Westlake ARPS.

The dinghy in which we so nearly lost our lives due to an under-estimation of the offshore wind at night. The picture was taken in much the same position as we were in at the time. *Chapter 3*.

The late 'Chunky' M. G. Duff, owner of *Hoshi* before the formation of the Island Cruising Club, and a very fine seaman. *Chapter 6.*

Hard on the wind of the *Hoshi*. We always carried our boats on their beam ends gripped to the davits. Without her original lead keel she was always a bit tender. *Chapter 6.*

Hoshi (pronounced Ho-she) was built by Camper and Nicholson in 1909, LOA 72-ft plus bowsprit and 50 tons TM. Like the other club ship, *Provident*, she has been sailed by the Island Cruising Club for over thirty years. *Chapter 6*. Photo: Island Cruising Club.

Outward Bound Sea School ketch *Warspite* alongside in Aberdovey for a scrub and annual examination; a powerful vessel, the ex-*Bluebird* yacht. *Chapter 7*.

Maintaining ratlines in *Hoshi*. The throat and lower mainsail brails can be seen. *Chapter 8*.

Broken bowsprit in *Provident*. The two parbuckle lines are still rove in the centre. *Chapter 10*.

The 70-ft Brixham Trawler *Provident* was built in 1924. Owned nowadays by the Maritime Trust, she is sailed and cared for by the Island Cruising Club of Salcombe, Devon. *Chapter 10*. Photo: Ken Fraser.

The 24-ft *Orari*, in which I was knocked down and pinned by a violent squall taking aboard a dangerous volume of water before she was able to right herself. *Chapter 14*.

Another day and a different thunder squall, but it was just such a squall coming over a hot and windless sea that so nearly sank my little *Orari*. *Chapter 14.*

8

Death Wish

If you work as a charter yacht skipper or crew you get seatime in fast. A six-month season can be the equivalent of five years of weekend and occasional holiday cruising. In a big old gaff-rigged yacht with ripe sails and running gear, a dud engine, only one other hand who knows the score and a party of eight or more total beginners, experience is rammed home like stuffing into a turkey. Whether you profit from the experience at the same rate is another matter, but what you do learn about fast is 'people'.

That year my wife Joyce, who was mate/cook, and I had had a fairly rocky start largely due to a bit too much wind as usual, plus the fact that trying to steer novices from one urgent rope to the next was like army netball. Three weeks earlier we had had a shattering experience. Unknown to us, one of our crew had previously spent quite a lot of time as a patient in a hospital for mental disorders and as soon as he was discharged as fit he had made the decision to book with us (he had never sailed before) for a recuperative holiday.

The upshot of that had been awesome. He had been very seasick on the sail over to Guernsey and it unhinged him. We had a berth alongside in St Peter Port and from 3.00 a.m. onwards we had to deal with a severe schizophrenic who whooped and ran naked around the ship pursued by me and in due course the harbour night watchman, a doctor and a team of policemen who had arrived in an ambulance. Of course, it wasn't funny, it was a grim thing. On the other hand, being mistaken for God (I had the makings of a beard) and standing guard over our engine, which he was determined to dismantle, had its moments.

That had been three weeks earlier. Now we had a new crew of novices joining for a gentle one-week cruise down the south Devon coast and back.

Francis was a small man in a state of high excitement which I attributed to nervousness. He did everything at the double, whistling shrilly throughout and racing around the schooner in the baggy shorts which were *de rigueur* in those days as if pursued by the hounds of hell – which in a sense he was. We were due to sail in about two hours' time when he sought me out for a quiet word.

'I have to tell you this out of fairness,' he said, 'but nobody else must know. The fact is that at some stage during the coming week I shall commit suicide.'

I couldn't believe it. This just could not happen. 'I'm quite determined,' he went on, 'I am booked to enter a mental hospital a few days after this cruise is due to finish and I can't face it – in fact, I don't have to face it . . .' There was a good deal more in the same vein. Nothing I could say, no amount of reasoning and pleading would budge him. And this just three weeks after the other . . .

I rowed ashore and found a doctor. He listened, then sighed and shook his head. 'There is nothing you or I can do,' he explained. 'Until such time as a person is committed (that's to say, detained for treatment because his behaviour constitutes a risk to society) he remains free to do as he pleases. After all, this may well be no more than talk – a desire for attention. Meanwhile, he has booked a holiday with you and his money is as good as the next man's.' The doctor told me to keep a sharp eye on him, which was tantamount to a housewife vacuuming the carpet while watching that the milk doesn't boil over. I returned aboard no happier.

The rest of the crew was a mixed bag of ages and sexes, but it included one man (whom we may as well call Tom) who had sailed with us on a couple of occasions in the past. He was stolid and on the face of things reliable. He at least knew the routines and the ropes. We sailed on the tide, when the stream outside was still foul but soon to turn westward, and our first goal was Fowey about thirty miles away from Salcombe. It was a hot, calm day for once and with a reaching breeze offshore.

Francis barely waited until we had cleared Salcombe bar before he began his antics. Singing stridently, he began tightrope-walking the bowsprit while I bellowed at him to get back inboard and stop acting the fool. He winked at me. Then he turned to the mainmast ratlines. 'Francis,' I said, 'you're not to go aloft. That's an order!'

As skipper my order should have been enough. Usually my crews accepted that and, grumble though they might, obey they would. If somebody refused an order, though, there wasn't a damn thing I could do about it at sea and Francis just ignored me and began to climb aloft. The main crosstrees were a favourite spot with these crews because, with the schooner heeling a little, it was an easy climb and the view and sense of soaring movement up there was delightful in quiet weather – for normal people.

Singing and clowning, Francis climbed while those below laughed at his antics. I watched, dry of mouth. Joyce, who knew the situation of course, had her hands clenched. Francis stood up there, forty feet above us, still clowning around but silently now. Then he stood for a long time looking down.

'For Christ's sake, Francis,' I begged him.

Schooners have a triatic stay. It is very heavy and it runs from fore to mainmast, bracing the two. Francis reached for it, leaned out and then, hand over hand, he swung himself through space, legs kicking wildly, traversing the void from one mast to the other. People on deck were cheering him on. I could only watch in horror. Half way he paused, dangling, then he continued on his way and reached the foremast. There were no ratlines on the foremast. He descended to the deck in the fashion natural to gaff-rigged craft, by using the ash mast hoops as steps. He landed on the deck and bowed to his audience, then I saw the sweat on his face and the tremor of his mouth as he gave a ghastly sort of smile. He went below to his bunk and there he remained. I felt a huge sense of relief but I wondered if it was only a reprieve. I wondered what else he would try later – we had a whole week of this ahead. Would he, one day, summon the courage to kill himself?

By mid-afternoon we were motoring. The ancient Gray petrol engine developed about twenty of its rated forty hp and pushed us along in quiet water at about four knots. In due course, as the day cooled, a small breeze returned from the land and, petrol still being rationed at that time, I cut the engine. We arrived off the entrance to Fowey at dusk. The wind was funnelling dead out of the narrow river with its high bluffs on either side, but I didn't much fancy short tacking with a raw crew and I decided to motor in. A big gaff schooner with her long keel doesn't tack like a small modern yacht. She has to be *sailed* round. You take her round in a wide, slow arc, using her weight to carry her through the eye of the wind, backing her headsails and if necessary reversing the rudder should she begin to make a sternboard. You can't afford to miss stays because there won't be time for a second try, not in a narrow rock-fringed entrance. The engine refused to start.

This was familiar enough. If the engine was still hot or even warm, there was often trouble. Sometimes it would pick up at once; at other times no amount of cleaning plugs and messing with the choke would help and no engineer ever cured the fault or even explained it. I bore off clear of trouble, hove to and spent an hour vainly trying to get it going, but to no avail. It was almost dark. Hoping for a fair slant, I had another go at short tacking but by then the ebb was beginning to run. I decided to make for Falmouth.

The breeze meanwhile was freshening and the sky had clouded over. The barometer fell sharply, but partly as a result, I guessed, of the normal diurnal rise-and-fall tendency. Falmouth lay twenty miles further west and its wide entrance and extensive sheltered anchorage made it attractive – the more so as, with the wind broad on our starboard beam, we were roaring across the flat, calm bay at nearly nine knots and there was every prospect of being in and at anchor soon after midnight. It is sheer lunacy for any sailing man to count chickens on a tally of eggs, especially the clutch of pot eggs I was counting.

I suppose that a small depression over northern France might have done it, or a front giving force 6–7 northerlies combining with that hot offshore thermal to produce a local gale. At all events, we had not reached Dodman Point before we had the gaff foresail and the jib off her and we were still over-pressed. In those days *Hoshi* needed a good deal more ballast in her and she was (and still is) tender. That the old lady is still sailing a full club season at the age of seventy-five is due to the excellent maintenance she gets plus the fact that her original lead keel, which made her as stiff as a tea chest full of books, has been replaced by a greenheart one and internal ballast. Without this and with the intensive use she has had during the past thirty years, she would have shaken herself to bits by now.

Hoshi was rigged with a standing main gaff at the time. In effect the gaff stayed aloft permanently and the mainsail was brailed in to the mast to stow it, like that of a Thames sailing barge. The aim had been to cut down on heavy sail handling for novice crews, but the arrangement created more problems than it solved, especially if you tried to brail up with the wind on or abaft the beam. What with main, upper and lower brails, vangs, a clew outhaul and clew outhaul purchase in addition to the existing throat and peak halyards and *their* purchases, it was not an easy sail to reef. To shift the outhaul to the next clew cringle meant partly lowering the whole outfit. If things got that bad we brailed up completely and sailed under gaff foresail or we set the main trysail.

For a while, then, we tore through a totally black night under full mainsail and staysail. The bow waves and the wake were so vividly phosphorescent that waves of light flowed up the sails and over the faces of those on deck, giving them an eerie corpse-like appearance which cheered me up no end, apprehensive about Francis as I was and what he might do now that it was dark. As we came up with St Anthony's Light, some five miles off, we met rough water. There had been a steady increase of sea since we had hit the tidal overfalls earlier but now, laid hard over under the offshore wind, we began leaping like some huge, glimmering salmon, spray like a gunshot bursting up from our bows as the bowsprit lashed the wave crests. I knew well enough that it was time to slow her. We were hard on the wind now, trying to shape up for the entrance to Falmouth. Suddenly there came a loud crack followed by utter, dangerous chaos.

The main boom fractured halfway along its thirty-foot length. It made a dog-leg which the flogging of the sail flailed around the deck and lee guardrail. The noise, the battering wind, yelling voices and the urgent threat of injury to someone gave me a dozen problems to solve at once. Joyce got spare hands (which was about everybody) off the decks and safely below, while I tried to clear a numbed brain. 'It's all right, there's nothing to worry about. Just keep your bloody heads down!' I yelled.

In the dark, in rough water and with only Joyce and Tom to help, it took over an hour to sort out the mess; the mainsail couldn't be brailed because the clew outhaul was hopelessly tangled with the broken boom and the whole sail had to be lowered and somehow secured. We had all sail off her at last. I gave up the notion of setting the main trysail with its mast lacing and two heavy gun tackles on wire pendants that served as sheets and instead set the gaff foresail again and, lashing the wheel up, let her lie-to. By that time we were many miles offshore in big seas. The lights of Falmouth were a glow on the underbellies of racing clouds. Joyce made us a hot drink.

We were in the big-ship lane. Our paraffin navigation lights were poor and it was before the days of radar reflectors. Now and again, belts of drizzly rain chopped visibility to a few hundred yards. I didn't even consider the engine. Even if I could start it, the feeble thrust it gave would not even turn her through the wind should I need to manoeuvre in an emergency. So I settled to keep watch and hope.

At first Joyce and Tom kept watch with me, then I sent her below to rest. It had been a long day. Tom began complaining. He was cold, the boom should never have broken, he hadn't paid for this sort of thing, etc. With hindsight I now realize that Tom was a frightened man. Nothing in his past life had prepared him for this bedlam of wind, water and crisis. His complaining pugnacity was a defensive measure. When I told him to go below and get his head down he did just that. It was then that I became aware of my arch problem, Francis.

He was standing against the doghouse looking around, having just come up from below. There was something odd, *odder* about him. The crazy, suicidal acrobat had gone, as had the wild-eyed paranoid of earlier. He sat on the coaming by me at the wheel. 'I know nothing about boats,' he said, 'but I get a feeling that we're in a bit of a tight spot. I was eavesdropping you see. I heard you goin' on about drifting into the way of big ships and that.' His voice was sober and concerned but there was no trace of either fear or hysteria about it. I told him the score just as it was. We were disabled, drifting offshore in a gale that showed no signs of any moderation and I was as worried as hell about shipping and about getting back into the lee of the land. 'Right, then,' he said. 'Tell me roughly where ships might come from, so that I can keep an eye open. Then you get into that dog kennel or whatever you call it and have a smoke.' I was desperately tired and drained. The doghouse was an open-ended structure right by where we were sitting, but it gave shelter from the wind and peace of a sort. Suddenly it was the most desirable place on earth. Suddenly also I felt that I had a man with me upon whom I could rely, a *different* man. I reached for my pipe.

Between us we saw the rest of that night out. Joyce woke and brewed strong coffee for us and we sat there on watch with the blackness paler as dawn came and the hissing seas that rose and fell around us taking on shape and size. Once a ship had appeared and towered close in an aura of hazy lights.

When it was light we began to work. Under foresail alone there had been no chance of working to windward successfully but now, with the help of Francis, Joyce and in due course the still-grumbling Tom, I sorted out the mess of ropes and got the main trysail on her. It took about two hours of lugging and cursing, every simple operation rendered one hundredfold more difficult by the rolling, jerking motion and by the apathy of exhaustion. Finally we set the staysail and I got the engine running, without difficulty on this occasion.

It was late afternoon by the time we dragged the poor old schooner into the shelter of the land and by then the wind had fallen and shifted to give us a long fetch into harbour. We anchored.

I was utterly and totally exhausted. I fell on my bunk and went to sleep. Joyce had the rest of the crew at work sorting out the mess, but Francis had his own plans. He had heard me say that the club would have to be phoned, and the coastguard, in case anyone ashore had reported our plight. He got a dinghy swung out and rowed ashore. He took over with an energy and efficiency that had the wheels in motion within an hour of our arrival and a replacement boom was already in hand by the time he was back aboard. I had awoken by then and he beckoned me to walk forward and join him by the bowsprit.

'I have just this to say,' he told me. 'What happened out there was what I needed. Forget whatever I said before. When the week is up I shall go into that hospital and have whatever treatment I'm due for, but I reckon it's just a waste of brass, skipper. I'm cured!'

The rest of the week, after a couple of days in Falmouth, left time for no more than a gentle sail into Helford and then home to Salcombe. I never saw or heard of Francis again.

Conclusions

In quiet weather all swans are swans and the geese don't appear until the going gets rough – which is when you get the surprises. Unless you know a person, or he comes to you with a recommendation from someone whose judgement you can trust, it is risky to base the crewing strength of a small yacht upon fine-weather performance.

Francis of course was a unique case, but not *that* unique. I once had a sleepwalker in the crew, a man who was recovering from a car crash and whose disturbing tendencies didn't surface until we were two nights out of Chichester *en route* for Ushant. On both nights, when supposedly off-watch, he emerged from the forehatch and wandered aft in his pyjamas, looked at the compass and wandered back again. We had no inkling that he was fast asleep. There was another man so steeped in book lore and so romantically in love with the sea that he could quote the Rules for Avoiding Collision word-perfect, make every knot, hitch and bend in the book and send Morse at near-professional speed. We hit bad weather soon after leaving harbour – just rough weather, no gale – and he became progressively sicker and more terrified, until he just lay in his bunk and *wept*. It was one of the saddest incidents of my sailing life.

Every skipper looks at his crew and mentally divides it into 'crew' and 'passenger' lists – or if he doesn't, he should. To cruise with a crew of tough experts is a joy. A skipper can go off watch and relax in the knowledge that the ship is in good hands, the ship can be sailed faster and further and the crew moreover probably *expect* her to be. Sailing with a party of friends or good companions isn't always synonymous with expert crewing, though, but cruising is like that. If the crew is weak in expertise or strength or fitness, there is always the anchorage near to home where you can watch the sun go down with a drink in your hand and there's nothing wrong with that.

What is disturbing is that unknown people have a way of changing roles according to conditions. It has happened again and again. The crewman you have relied upon during sail changes, handling ship when entering a dock, coming up to anchor, furling and stowing; the crewman who has read exhaustively and been to sailing schools, taken his tests and put his seatime in may *still* not yet have stood the real test and you don't know it and neither does he. The other chap, useless and in everybody's way, suddenly emerges as the tower of strength and fortitude upon whom you rely when everybody else has long since succumbed to exhaustion. For that matter, a skipper cannot always be sure that he himself may not one day become a passenger. He gets older, less fit perhaps, and years go by without anything happening to put him to the test. Sure as hell it will happen, if he keeps at it long enough, and when it does, will he be up to it?

These are imponderable questions. There are no guidelines, no guarantee that the novice pain-in-the-butt will become a hero as soon as the wind begins to pipe or that the ball of fire who is such an excellent crew is going to fold on you. You rarely know the background story of a chance crew. Neither do you know a person's medical history and who would ever suggest that a guest for a quiet weekend cruise should be asked to declare the state of his appendix? What we can do is regard casual crew as being *extra*. If the ship needs two fully competent people to manage her at sea, that is what she must have – or stick to safe and gentle sailing. I have been in the situation of looking around at ten recumbent, moaning forms and wondering how the hell to get sail off the ship. Joyce and I once ran the ship for miles until there was room to gybe her round after lowering the main peak simply because there was nobody left to handle the headsail sheets.

The alternative is to become an expert at singlehanded sailing.

Note: Looking back: no, he would never have done it and the doctor had been right. Francis was a lonely and frightened man who just needed to have somebody to care about him and be concerned. I am in danger of sounding like a DIY psychologist, but it seems that a hell of a lot of people who behave in one extreme manner or another are just people who either need human attention or something big to measure themselves up against.

9

No Shelter

The old Falmouth Quay Punt came trundling into Salcombe on top of a big spring tide. She got halfway through a slow and lazy tack and, upright for a moment, her long keel touched in the shallows and there she stuck.

This was unremarkable enough. Seamen have been running aground down the centuries. 'We're *on!*' they have chorused in a thousand languages. Richard followed the time-honoured ritual of heeling the vessel, backing sails, sugging her (rocking her on her keel) and finally lowering sails and resorting to the engine, which did no good either, for by then the ebb was away.

Built originally to serve as a shore link for the big square riggers lying in Falmouth's Carrick Roads, the Quay Punt was around thirty feet in length and her deep hull with its long keel drew nearly six feet aft. On the face of it, though there wasn't much to worry about because her grounding in Mill Bay was well inside the estuary of Salcombe, inside the bar and sheltered to east and west by steep, high ground. The only problem was grounding on top of a spring tide, and plainly there would be a bit of a struggle to get her off on the next tide during the night.

Richard was a friend of ours and as the tide left his boat we went down to lend a hand with laying out her anchor towards deep water. She was lying with her bows towards the shore, so we ran the warp through her quarter fairlead after running it outside all: when she began to float, this would keep her from going further on until we were ready to swing and haul her off. To pass the time we gave her a scrub. Holidaymakers on the sands watched and munched sandwiches while their youngsters dug holes nearby. Richard borrowed one of their spades and began to dig a keel trench towards deep water until the infant began to bawl blue murder when he returned the toy spade in some haste. The sky began to cloud over.

'I don't know,' Richard said, 'it might not be a bad idea to get a launch laid on for tonight. It doesn't look all that cheerful and she's got to come off or stay here another ten days or more.' We agreed. Nothing bad was forecast, only a freshening breeze and a bit of rain because of a front going through, but you never knew, did you?

By dusk that evening, and with the tide flooding, Richard, his girlfriend Helen and I had taken station aboard to wait. A local harbour launch had been laid on to assist at around high water. There was a mean little wind out of the south-west, tending a bit southerly, which is the direction from which Salcombe bar is wide open; a very mean little wind that fretted and hummed in the rigging and came cat's-pawing across the water, carrying with it the thin Devonian rain in hanging drapes. 'Blast this,' Richard said. 'Let's get below and have a drink.'

As was to be expected, the Quay Punt lay at an angle of about thirty or more degrees, but we sat in a row on the port settee with our knees in the air. What with the gin bottle in regular play and our pipes going nicely, the time passed pleasantly. We were well down the bottle when we heard the first bum-smack of a wavelet hitting the bilge and the suckings and gurglings of the returning tide. A seacock made a rude noise. We listened, aware also that the sound of the wind had increased a lot. 'We're going to need that launch,' I said. Richard slid back the hatch and looked out. The wind came tearing past him into the cabin, bringing the rain. He could see to windward a corrugation of white wavelets in the moonlight that filtered through flying cloud. Beyond the constant hiss of the wavelets we could all hear the deep bass booming of the harbour bar. He shut the hatch again. The old boat gave a sudden lurch as her bilges lifted and fell.

We drank some more but our minds were not on it and we wished we'd been a little less prodigal earlier. The noise was louder and the old craft was lifting and slamming her bilge regularly now. The gravel was grinding under her and her fifty-year-old timbers and planks creaked painfully. We couldn't sit there any longer.

Outside in the cockpit we stared at a gingerish full moon racing through ragged cloud. The Quay Punt was almost on her feet and taking the punishment on her keel, which was some relief, but to windward the wavelets had become rollers that advanced and burst upon us, slamming the flat transom to deluge us almost without cease. Our anchor rope began to slam taut as the old boat came afloat and lunged shorewards. We would have slipped and tried to turn her on it, but the launch had arrived.

It was hopeless from the start. With the sea and boats there are times when it is quite plain that a particular strategy is not going to work, and yet you keep on at it. It was a smaller launch than we'd expected and with only one man in her. Moreover she was beam-on to the wind and sea as she closed us and being a long, narrow craft she was not to be turned easily upwind. However, the tow-line was passed and the strain was taken. Within seconds the launch had fallen off in the trough, girt by our line, and the launchman predictably let go in a hurry. He made three attempts and then gave us the wash-out signal and made off home.

Richard was cursing at the top of his voice. He pointed at the water just ahead of our bows and I saw what he meant. The seas were breaking with the solid weight of waves meeting a steep beach and I remembered that the beach rose steadily just there. He pointed at our straining anchor warp and screamed in my ear, 'Can't slip . . . get her heel aground . . . if she swings. . . .'

So we stayed as we were, stern to sea, afloat and lungeing at the warp in wind-whipped explosions of spray. Richard started the engine and put it full astern, hoping to relieve the strain, but after a short while it spluttered and stopped. The filler cap on the transom had somehow come off and the tank must have been half-filled with seawater. He made a gesture of hopelessness and pointed at the companionway, I nodded and followed him and Helen below.

'We'll just have to sit it out and wait for the ebb, that's all. At least we're out of it,' he said, still shouting for it was bedlam even down there. He found the gin bottle and we took up where we'd left off. It was not a party I'd ever want to attend again. The boat gyrated insanely, dropping into a trough only to surge forwards and bring up with a neck-breaking shock as the anchor warp slammed taut, then the rumble and roar of surf exploding forwards around us. It was plain that things couldn't stay that way for long and even if the warp held there was the ebb to come when she'd take the ground again.

Then we heard a sound like an express train and the stern tilted upwards and rose sharply just as the breaker struck and engulfed us. The companionway had little hinged doors and these burst inwards under a wall of solid water which cascaded upon us, filling our gin glasses and filling the saloon to the level of the settees where we sat. Before we could reach the cockpit we heard another one coming and we felt the sluggish rise of the now half-filled hull.

That the anchor had dragged was plain, for the breakers were all around us and we could feel her hitting the beach. We had to get the hell off and ashore. Richard was shouting. 'Helen . . . can't swim . . . line ashore. . . .' We had no lifejackets. If there were any lifebuoys, none was in evidence. In those days neither of these aids was taken very seriously, but I was serious enough by that time. If Helen couldn't swim, yes we'd need a lifeline to the shore with someone ashore to haul her in. Who was to take the line ashore?

'I'll . . . swim . . . ashore!' I shouted, not too loudly in case he heard me. But he had heard me. 'No,' Richard screamed, '. . . my girl . . . ship. . . .' I backed down with honour saved and a feeling of relief.

Looking shorewards in the light of the racing moon was no comforting sight. There seemed to be a good hundred yards of breaking water, a white maelstrom of churning and smoking spray. The old boat was slamming the beach in every trough and due to fall apart like a wet cigar box any second. Richard made a bowline around his waist. He had bent on every spare line he could lay hands on. Suddenly he had gone and I was paying out frantically. With dread in my heart I stared for a sight of him, then I saw him flailing like a harvester.

In a moment of moonlight I could see him standing up and he was leaping around and waving idiotically. It seemed uncalled for to exhibit such pride in achievement. Then I secured the line around Helen's waist, making a job of it, and with tremendous courage for a non-swimmer she took a deep breath and jumped. She seemed to plane along the surface as Richard heaved. Then she too was safely ashore and it was my turn. I recommended my soul to the Almighty as if it was some of sort of bargain offer, then I jumped.

I stood up. The water was a little under waist-deep. I could have swum if I had gone in flat like Richard but I'd jumped and that was why he'd been waving so idiotically. I waded ashore, leaving the old Punt to hammer herself to pieces against the steep ledge of the beach.

By daylight she was strewn all over the beach like firewood.

Conclusions

A good strong element of farce doesn't hide the fact that this was potentially a very dangerous little adventure and it raises some interesting angles – the question of shelter in tidal waters, for instance.

In many places, what appears to be a sheltered creek on the chart becomes a huge expanse of open water at high tide, and although in the steep-to waters of the Salcombe anchorage this was not so much the case, the rising level did mean that the bar and the normally protective rocky outcrops at the mouth of the harbour were less of a barrier against the open sea. A heavy swell would have been running in.

With the wind blowing full ashore in our little bay, the fetch across the harbour was half a mile at the most. Fetch, the distance which wind can blow unimpeded across open water, generates wind-driven waves of a height relative to wind strength. A wind of, say, force 7–8 (33–36 knots) might raise a sea of twelve to fifteen feet in height in open water. It could well have raised a four- to five-foot sea on our lee shore, but what made it dangerous was the big cross swell that was running in. Additionally, the steep-to beach was causing the waves to plunge, they were tripping forward on a rising seabed and breaking violently. To anchor in harbour is one thing, but for a small boat a lee shore in harbour can still be dangerous enough to wreck her.

The anchor we laid off was an ordinary Fisherman type, but we knew enough to lay it out on the longest scope we could reach. I believe we bent a warp on to the bitter end of the chain, a total of forty fathoms. We also dug the anchor in so that it had a maximum hold from the first moment of strain. Had it needed to drag some way before getting a full bite, our Quay Punt would have been in the breaker line from the start and might have broken up much sooner. The seabed was solid sand, but it seems likely that the anchor settled behind a buried stone. Otherwise, I am sure it would have dragged earlier. A Fisherman, unlike a plough or other burying anchor which builds up holding power as the load causes it to go deeper, reaches a maximum hold quickly but its hold is not one-quarter that of a burier of the same weight. Moreover, once it begins to drag there's no stopping it – unless the dragging is due to the scope being too short, when veering extra scope will stop it, at least temporarily.

There was no way we could have hauled off by that anchor without a windlass. In any case, the surge loads would probably have wrecked a small one. Even by hauling in the lulls between waves the need to hold fast with a turn for each oncoming sea would have made it highly dangerous. Had she been bows-on it might have been possible, but not by manpower alone.

The abortive attempt by the launch reflects no discredit on the launchman, only an ability to sum up the situation quickly as hopeless. Even if he had been able to assume a bows-to-sea attitude, the fact that the tow was made fast to his stern would have defeated him. His launch would have been brought up all-standing by the load, a sea would have thrown his bows aside and he would have been beam-on again in seconds.

The tow must be made fast well forward so that the stern is free to traverse from side to side as the helm is altered to hold her head to sea. This calls for a towing post up in the bows otherwise the tow-rope will sweep athwart the boat and foul the engine box or rudder head – even if the launchman can manage to keep ducking underneath it. If the wind had not been dead on shore, it might have been possible to tow *on a sheer* – that is to say, with the rope attached to one side of the launch well forward, leading clear of everything to the wreck which would be on her quarter. The launch would have been able to lie head to wind and the stern would have had a limited arc of swing. It is doubtful, though, whether this would have been a success. It is wise to be suspicious of any tow-off attempt with the rope attached to the stern unless the rescue craft is a big, heavy and powerful one or the conditions are less severe.

The hammering a beached hull must take as the tide refloats her may sound worse than it is and much depends on the slope of the beach. If it is a very flat, gradual slope, the first breakers will be so small that they merely slap the bilges. If only a couple of feet of water or less is all that is needed to allow the boat to begin to lift, the waves may remain small enough to be harmless, although the scrunching sounds echoing through the hull will be terrifying. If the beach is steep-to, though, the tide edge advances slowly with a line of weighty breakers which lift the bilge and drop it heavily.

Once the boat begins to rise, although still on her keel, she will slew broadside to the waves unless she has an anchor out to stop her. Then the real damage may be done as she lifts and crashes down, with the whip of the mast adding to the violence – hence the need to lay off an anchor to windward, whatever the circumstances of grounding. A ten-hour wait for the returning tide allows time for some radical changes in the weather, as we found out.

Just how much pounding a boat can stand must depend upon the builder and the type of hull construction. A traditional wooden boat soon begins to crack rib timbers if left on her bilge, then plank seams open up and she begins to take in water. Oddly enough, if the boat sinks where she lies she can sometimes be saved from total destruction because, no longer able to lift and fall, the seas break against her as they might against a rock. All then depends upon the weight of the seas.

A wooden hull pounding on her keel is taking the punishment on her strongest component and the structure of floors, frames and bulkheads distribute the shocks. Such a keel, with its massive deadwood, can take fearful hammering. A GRP hull may have a hollow box or keel trough which lacks this solidity, moreover the ceaseless grinding and slamming against a rough seabed can chew away the layers of glassfibre and loosen the moulded-in ballast. On the other hand, a well-built GRP hull with the heavy lay-up around the keel and moulded reinforcement floors above it does a good job of dispersing the shocks. What must be remembered, though, is that no builder builds specifically with hammering on a lee shore in mind and if he did so few buyers would be willing to foot the bill for the extra glass and resin that went into the construction.

The denouement of my story, the waist-deep wade ashore, masks a sober question. How does one get ashore in surf? Joyce and I once went swimming in the Azores before the return leg of the AZAB race. The island of São Miguel has few places where it is possible to swim, but we had seen locals swimming on this particular beach of black volcanic sand and we didn't think twice. The beach was very steep-to. The waves came riding in, built up high within perhaps fifty yards of the beach edge and then crashed forwards. Joyce was in difficulties at once. At first it seemed funny. Her feet were swept from under her by a spent wave as it ran back and she was hurled forward by the following breaker. I went to her aid and became powerless. Together we were slammed down, stunned, rolled and sucked back again and again. When we finally dragged ourselves out we were bruised, dazed and very frightened.

That is the effect of undertow on a quiet day. On a steep beach the mass of returning water along with tons of loose sand or gravel make keeping your feet next to impossible and the incoming plungers overwhelm you. There is no water to swim in, only foam and gravel. When swimming in such conditions, you must dive through the first line of breakers and swim strongly seawards but we didn't know this.

Seen from a stranded boat in danger of breaking up, the backs of plunging breakers look far less dangerous than they may be. The advice that a crew should stay on the wreck as long as possible is unquestionably good, although the violence of motion, the almost continual blast of heavy spray and possibly even solid water, plus the sheer noise, can induce people to make a try for the shore.

We had no distress signals but if we had been able to signal our plight, there would almost surely have been help, at least on the beach. Whether it would have been professional help is another matter. In a real emergency (ours was a seeming emergency) a bunch of holidaymakers, unskilled in rescue and their efforts uncoordinated, might give more aid to morale than physical help. In surf of the kind we met on that Azores beach just two or three people linking hands could have got us out, but two or three people plunging in separately would have joined us on their faces.

It is questionable whether it is a sensible solution for one person to make a bid for the shore carrying a lifeline. Much depends upon the collective swimming ability of the group, and a crew roped together and wearing the vital lifejackets would probably stand a better chance, although the possibility of a swimmer falling foul of the connecting rope exists. No rules can be formulated except the basic one about staying with the wreck for as long as humanly possible.

10

Provident

It was an Easter cruise. *Hoshi*, my usual command, was still being fitted out and I was given the Brixham trawler *Provident* for a long weekend to the Channel Islands, a first sail of the season and a shake-down cruise which was to shake me to my tripes.

We were due to sail on Friday but a series of early gales had only just begun to moderate a little and I delayed until the tide on the following day. Outside Salcombe the wind was sou'westerly, giving a broad fetch for Les Hanois with a big loutish sea forward of our starboard beam that hit and burst with clouds of icy spray across our heeling decks. A Brixham trawler with a reef under her topsail and working headsails is a powerful sailer with the wind a shade free and we thrust seawards with lee shrouds slack and idle, halyards standing in taut curves to compliment the drum-hard curves of the sails. Slam-bang we went, ironwork jangling and galley pans clattering below: fine stirring sailing, the very thing for which our crew had signed on. They lay moaning with pleasure along the lee bulwarks.

After some hours of this fine sailing, the wind backed a shade southerly and began to freshen. Prudently I took the topsail off her which left her a bit under canvased, but now, hard on the wind, she felt better. It backed a bit more and I laid off a course for the north of Guernsey so that we'd have a bit of lee for the run up the Little Russel. We never got that far.

It was late afternoon and Casquets lay about fifteen miles due east when there was a sharp report from forward and a sudden great racket of flogging sails and general maritime mayhem.

The students of our lee quarter wave turned ravaged vellum-coloured faces bow-wards. The starboard bowsprit shroud had parted, the bowsprit bent incredibly and then broke hard by the gammon to whip leewards in a tangle of sail and gear. Moments later I heard an answering crack from aloft as the lee crosstree, fouled by the topmost forestay, also snapped off. Everybody rushed forward to have a look, the hale and the walking wounded alike. 'Heave her to, quick!' I ordered, shouldering through the spectators.

We hove to by backing the staysail and easing the main, then I slipped a becket on the wheel and took stock again. The bowsprit, around thirty-five feet by ten inches thick of solid fir, was alongside our lee topsides hammering and pounding like Santa's workshop. Its ironwork was grinding into our topside planking and was painful to watch. As we rolled up and over the rising sea, now on our beam, the spar would step back and then slam into us with horrifying force; something needed to be done in a hurry. My first thought was to disentangle the mess of rope and wire so that the broken spar could be streamed astern, but I quickly gave up that attempt. We tried lifting one end at a time, but it was far beyond our strength.

So we parbuckled. The mate and I, with our wives hanging on to our oilskins as we leaned over the side, managed to pass two lines down outwards under the spar and back aboard, one aft and the other by the lee shrouds. Then, with all hands tailing on, we rolled it up our topsides and secured it along the rail. By the time we'd finished it was dark. There was no other shipping about so we all trooped below, ruddy faced and triumphant, to find that Harry, the club secretary, had got the fire going and had had the infinite wisdom to put potatoes in the oven early on in the game. Morale soared; sickness had fled from all except for one little man, about whom more later.

What I would have to do, I decided, was start the engine and motorsail the remaining miles until we were under the lee of the island. It was a simple decision crisply made, as rich in hope as Leonardo da Vinci's flying machine and equally fated to failure – he had his sums wrong and I hadn't reckoned on the rocking-horse motion of a ship hove-to in a tumble of sea.

Our engine, in its own engine room, was a big diesel of German origin and said to have been a tank engine. Hitherto it had given no trouble apart from responding better when starting cold to having a lighted paraffin rag stuck up its chuff. This time there was not a sign of life in it, no matter what fiery inducement I offered to its air intake. It was coldly and utterly dead. Various experts had a go since my knowledge of diesels stopped at the starter button, but all they did was to run the battery completely flat.

I spent the rest of the night running the charger until the battery had guts enough to turn the engine over then, having turned it over to no avail, charging again. We lay hove-to hour after hour while the wind blew a rainy force 7–8 and our long trawler counter slammed and rose, slammed and rose as we rocking-horsed over the seas. That was the answer. I didn't know it, though, until much later when Brixham engineers lifted the engine head and found it full of seawater siphoned back up the stern-exiting exhaust pipe.

Sunday morning dawned wild and troubled with the radio warning of further gales on the way. It was only a weekend cruise anyway and while there might be time to reach St Peter Port it was hardly worth the risk of becoming gale-bound there. We drew sheets and headed *Provident* back to Brixham.

There was a sad note to that cruise. One of the crew members who was a stranger to me was a small meek man who had never in his life been to sea and yet who had an aching, burning passion for everything to do with sail and ocean. He had read every book he could find, every classic, until he could quote Conrad and the rest by the page. He could read the flags and rattle off morse. He knew the Rules of the Road inside out and, with a rope's end in hand, he could make every knot, bend and hitch there was. He had never been afloat, though, and from the outset he had become paralytically seasick and stiff with fright, taking to his bunk and lying whimpering there until the moment we slid into the shelter of Brixham. Then he dressed, packed and hurried ashore, there to begin formal complaints against me for my incompetence in endangering the ship. What happened to him, I often wonder? What about his dream?

Conclusions

When the bowsprit shroud parted we later found that a shackle pin was the culprit – or rather we were. So often when linking up shrouds of any sort, the shackles are chosen because the size happens to fit an eye. The fact that a bigger size of shackle should have been used, and if necessary a larger eye in proportion to the working load of the wire, gets lost in the haste to finish the job. The handy shackle that happens to fit becomes a weak link.

I was highly delighted with myself over the parbuckling operation, never having tried it in deadly earnest before. Dismasting can happen to anybody and recovering what is left of the spar is not always made easier by reason of having an alloy mast instead of a solid log.

Years later, when crewing in a race, we were dismasted because one crosstree had become kinked before the race (possibly by some

unknown boat berthing alongside clumsily) and although the
weather wasn't at all bad the kinked cross tree suddenly collapsed
and overboard went the mast from just above deck level, it being a
keel-stepped spar. On that occasion we had all hell's delight getting
the spar back aboard because it was full of water and the upper part
of it had to be raised high in order to drain it. With the wildly
increased motion, a lack of tools and no wire cutters, in those days it
took us almost two hours to sort out the mess and the parbuckling of
one end played a big part in the struggle.

In the case of *Provident* it was far easier once the very dangerous
stage of passing the lines under the bowsprit had been managed.

The siphoning back of water through the exhaust pipe is not
uncommon. It can happen to a small yacht in harbour if the owner
decides to give a party on deck and a ton or more of yakking human
beings overloads the stern. It need not happen if there is an adequate
swan-neck or a water trap properly placed in the exhaust line. At that
time in *Provident* the swan-neck was quite adequate for normal
sailing or for parties on deck, considering also the size and huge

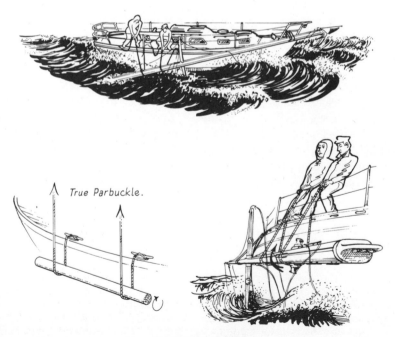

True Parbuckle.

So we parbuckled.

buoyancy of her hull; what it was not able to cope with was the pumping action of the rocking-horse motion.

Any vessel with a counter stern is liable to take a lot of punishment if she lies hove-to in a sea. Years ago off the west of Brittany there was a great loss of life in the sailing tunnyfishing fleet and I believe half the fleet of about twenty boats literally hammered themselves to pieces.

Tunnymen have long, flat counters and high bows. Hove-to, they slam their counters down with explosive force and, lying thus out in the open Atlantic for days on end while a storm of unusual severity continued without a let-up (and no doubt many of the boats were very old), they broke up and sank under the feet of their crews.

Even *Hoshi*, if hove-to for a night in anything of a seaway, perhaps waiting to enter an unlit river, would slam her tail down in this way. Later, we would find that the seam of every plank under her counter was visible where the hammering had started the line of stopping over the caulking. It wasn't serious – it was due to the natural 'give' of the planks and frames – but it was annoying after all the painstaking care that went into a glossy paint job.

More about *Provident*

We couldn't afford to let *Provident* lie idle for long – she was a working vessel and the summer season is brief. A new crosstree and bowsprit were soon provided, although once again they were fir instead of the original pitchpine – a fine, whippy, resinous timber that needed no shrouds at all in the old days* – and apart from the engine, which was still spouting seawater, we were ready for sea. The engine would not be ready for at least a month, we were told, new parts had to be imported and everything else stripped down and buffed up. 'But then,' said our commodore and founder, John Baylay, 'Brixham trawlers never used to have engines and this is a unique opportunity to turn the clock back by cruising without one.'

I regarded this unique opportunity with mixed emotions, which is

Note: In the days when Brixham trawlers fished for their living their bowsprits were of pitchpine and unstayed, some without even a bobstay, but then they were whippy spars that could be reefed. The fixed bowsprit of less flexible timber (it became very difficult to find pitchpine) needed shrouds and, because there was sometimes a need for a crew to climb out on it, the shrouds served as footropes too.

to say that the idea petrified me, not the actual sailing, of course, but the bumbling-around-in-tight-anchorages and the berthing-alongside bit. Brixham trawlers may have had no engines but they did have highly trained crews and skippers.

We sailed from Brixham, breaking clear on the right tack and fetching the end of the breakwater on the other. There is a penalty that goes with sailing a Brixham trawler in and out of Brixham. There is a row of indestructible old men who sit smacking their gums and wagging their heads as they watch every movement. 'Your mizzen,' they'd admonished once, 'should be first up and last down. You 'ad un dain afore ee was anchored!' I couldn't explain that the ten-thumbed mob which was crewing me that time had dropped the whole lot on my head as I stood at the wheel.

I remember little of the early part of that two-week cruise, so it must have gone smoothly. Vaguely I recall being becalmed in Alderney race with the old trawler spinning 360 degrees in the swirls and eddies, and I remember anchoring outside St Peter Port. We sailed west for Ushant thereafter with the Gulet de Brest and Cameret in mind, it being another place I reckoned I could do safely under sail.

There are two uneasy and contradictory features about any of the passages inside Ushant. One is the fact that if you can't see the next mark from the one you have just passed you had better keep your fingers crossed, and the other is the frequency of local fogs combined with wind. At spring tides the current in the Fromveau Channel can run at nine knots. We had a northerly following breeze when we closed the land with its countless rocks and reefs and perhaps it was by my holding so far off that I missed the inshore Chanal du Four, where the tides at springs only run at six or seven knots. Hence my assault on the Fromveau Channel.

To have even an unreliable engine aboard is of some comfort, false though it may be. When most of your engine lies under a tarpaulin on the quay in Brixham and a fair wind and tide are setting eighty tons of oak and pine towards a seemingly unbroken line of foam-wracked reefs, you feel a bit helpless. Your perfect navigator in an ideal world reads his pilotbook with calm care, looks carefully at his chart and then quietly cons the ship through a hazard-strewn channel without more ado. Not I: back and back again I trotted, searching the pilotbook with popping eyes, stabbing the chart with shaking fingers, then returning yet again to the wheel like a mating woodcock on its level flight. I had made the Du Four passage before but not the Fromveau. Every time I took a fresh look at the book I found something quite different, some new and awful warning, and I could imagine the writer of long ago shaking a mournful head as he penned the words. I was on the point of coming hard on the wind while we could still make an offing when I sighted the beacon tower I needed.

The tower came towards us as if it were on wheels. It had a bow-wave like a destroyer. The fog closed in as it came abeam. One minute I was looking at the marks ahead and the next moment they had gone. Simultaneously I realized that with such a tide under us the following wind (as in another episode described in this book) should have been reduced to a negligible apparent wind. It had been fresh before, yet now it was even fresher.

The Fromveau is in reality a simple channel if you can see where you are going and if you know the precise set of the current. If you know neither, dead reckoning is about as helpful as sending out a dove. On the stern capping we had a couple of flaked-out carrier pigeons hitching a ride in the wrong direction. I looked at them hopefully. We bored on into a blank wall, compass spinning as the kelds and eddies swung us. It was pointless to look at the chart any more, so I took the wheel to be ready to take frantic avoiding action.

'Look – there!' Abeam to port, just for a brief instant, we saw and heard the boil and commotion of a tooth of rock maybe a couple of lengths away. I felt my guts knotting up tight. 'Bring me the chart, someone,' I said, trying to sound calm. We must have been setting too much to the south-east. Either we were skating the edge of the mass of rocks on the eastern side of the channel or we were already *amongst* them. I asked the mate to take a sounding on the handlead, but he couldn't get bottom. I laid off to starboard a bit. I had been steering south-west and I made it south 70 west, thinking that there was now no way I could get fouled up on the rocks flanking Ushant Island to the west of us and that we would more likely be spat out into the Atlantic, there to wander in deep water until I had sorted out my navigational marbles.

There was a buoy that had figured in my earlier plans, the Pierres Verts, to be left to port before shaping in towards the entrance to the Gulet de Brest but which I could not now possibly hope to find on my new heading. It appeared instantly fine to port. Had I not altered when I had, we would have run straight into the reefs which it was there to guard. I knew, the mate knew and so did Joyce. 'Get ready to gybe,' I said.

The fog cleared soon afterwards and we ran on in quite safely. In that wind Cameret was out of the question, though, and I had an uneasy feeling that the harbour of Brest would be where we were bound, with all the complications of anchoring in an unknown place but with none of the second thoughts possible when you have an engine.

We anchored for the night in a sheltered bay just short of the Gulet (which had an ominous ring to it) with darkness fast approaching. The next morning we continued upriver under plain sail until the war-battered port and harbour of Brest opened up. Inside the breakwaters there was plenty of room, but I sailed up and down weighing up the anchorage and where best to lie for convenience in getting ashore, always a thing to take time over. I also had to think ahead in terms of getting out again under sail. Then I spotted a vacant berth alongside a quay and nicely dead to windward which looked a bit derelict and unlikely to be reserved. At the end of the berth was a blank wall.

It was to be the only time in my life that I berthed a big (by my standards) engineless craft under sail. The breeze was light and steady, calling for a short tack approach and a final long luff and shoot up. The question was, how long is a long luff and how much way does an eighty-ton heavy-displacement ketch carry? With twenty-odd feet of bowsprit stuck out and non-reefing, thanks to idiot yachtsman conversion, to overshoot at speed would chalk up two bowsprits lost inside a month. I mentally crossed myself. On the other hand, if I undershot I could either back her off, put in a sternboard and go out again, or anchor on short scope and warp her in.

We worked her closer in lazy tacks, making a final approach on port tack until, with three or four lengths to go, I brought her up. With the sails rustling and the sheets rapping, we glided on. Had the breeze been stronger I would have fallen short, but in that gentle breeze we just went on and on until I was starting to feel panic and some shore watchers were beginning to crouch in the way they do when an event is about to be enacted. *Provident* went another length and dropped alongside with scarcely a jar. I don't know whether it was impeccable seamanship or superlative luck. I'd have to try it on a regular basis to know the answer.

During the day another yacht came alongside. She was about fifty feet overall, her heavy spars were white-painted, she carried a twin pole Trade Wind rig and she had bag o' wrinkle hung about her like ivy on a church porch. I was to be given a decision to make that has intrigued me all my life. The yacht, I found from her Scottish skipper, was owned by a French company and she was outward bound on a voyage around the world, gathering material for a documentary film about seafolk, fishermen, folklore and underwater exploration. It seemed that one member of the crew had packed his bags and quit, leaving a vacancy. The skipper liked the way I had brought *Provident* in – he had watched from the anchorage – and he thought I would fit in with his crew very nicely, but they were leaving next morning and I had to make up my mind by then. I was three years married, with no children and no other ties. I didn't want to leave Joyce. Would she have ever forgiven me if I'd jumped ship? Could I have lived with my conscience? If I had gone, though, how might my life have panned out? I shall never know, but watching the yacht sail next morning was a heart wrench. I am glad I didn't go, but intrigued nonetheless.

The wind remained off the land and it was still light when we left. I put a backspring on her, dropped her aft until her stern overlapped the end of the wharf and then bore off forward on the boathook until we could get our jib aback, all very easy and smooth. Brest harbour had a second and eastern entrance and it seemed a good idea to go out that way just for fun. There must somewhere be a black book in which are recorded the good ideas tried just for fun and the electrifying results.

There was the usual bunch of anglers hunched over their rods on the end of the mole at the entrance and they eyed our approach with the prickly hostility which is common to pierhead anglers the world over. '*Attention, attention!*' they whooped in chorus, gesturing at their lines. I skirted them carefully, having once run off with a hook in the rudder leaving a cursing angler to mourn a whole reel of monofiliment, and we passed out into open water – or so we thought.

We had sailed a couple of cables when someone noticed the anglers all leaping up and down, waving in great agitation. I assumed we'd snared a hook and I took a look over the stern, but there was no sign of one and the water was clear. 'Listen, listen,' one of my crew said urgently. The anglers were shouting, in French of course. 'They're saying, "Back, back,"' he translated. 'They say something about *wrecks*!' I tore forward to the bows and stared at the water where I now saw that the surface ahead was rippling as though a shoal of sardines were mustering. 'Oh, hell's delight!' I gasped; then, tearing aft again, 'Sheet in quick, I'm coming round!'

We gybed her over and hardened in on a reciprocal beam reach, heading back for the eastern entrance again. I stared astern. It seemed that the whole of the area for which we had been heading was dark and disturbed-looking, yet the chart showed it to be free and linking with the main channel outside the harbour. We fetched the entrance again on the next tack and my linguist crew held a long conversation with the anglers who acted out in voice and clever mime the latter part of the Second World War complete with shot, shell and bombed and sinking ships: the obstructions we had almost hit.

Once back in the harbour, we found that the light breeze faded and died completely, yet out in the Rade we could see a breeze cat's-pawing the water. With an engine no problem would have existed, but to be stuck where we were would probably cost us the tide. We anchored short with the last of our steerage way.

I had heard about umbrella warping but I had never tried it. 'We're going to umbrella warp her,' I told the assembly. Later that cruise, in another calm over water too deep for what I proposed, we were to find that a boat lashed either side with two crew in each pulling the outboard oars could move her at over one knot, but that was still in the mists of the future and a rare treat yet in store for my crew. 'Get the boats down,' I ordered, 'and I want the two kedges and all the spare rope you can find bent together in one warp.'

Umbrella warping, which is a survival from the days of the sailing navies, is quite simple. You need a very long warp – the longer the better – with a kedge at each end. If you have two dinghies so much the better, but you begin by laying out one kedge ahead at the full extent of the warp with its other end leading in at one bow fairlead and out of the other dangling the second kedge. As the working party aboard hauls the ship up to her first kedge, the second one is being taken out ahead and it is let go as soon as the first breaks out, thus walking the ship along. In the days of sail it was probably resorted to if the breeze was too fresh for the ship's boats to tow her to windward, if that was the direction in which she had to be moved.

We kept it up for over half a mile and once *Provident* had way on her, as I had found when shooting into the berth, she kept going. In the end we were making a knot and a half. My crew were in the final throes of physical collapse but I urged them on cheerily, a quip here, a congratulation there, as I stepped over their croaking forms. 'This is living history,' I encouraged them. 'It may well be that no vessel has umbrella warped since the advent of steam at sea.' They were too choked with emotion by this fascinating conjecture to answer me.

The rest of the cruise was to be uneventful, save for the calm off Dartmouth when, with boats alongside, we towed her the four miles to round Berry Head, all in the sweltering heat of a hot and oppressive afternoon. We anchored inside the Head to await a breeze. Joyce made curry for supper.

Conclusions

In later years I was to own a little twenty-four-footer with an engine that almost drowned me (see the chapter entitled 'Beam Ends') and I took it out and stood it in the shed for the rest of that season and the following one. It could do less harm in my shed. Both the cruising in *Provident* and the engineless period in *Orari*, the twenty-four-footer, were high spots in my cruising life. The sheer fact of knowing that you don't have an engine alters your whole concept of sailing. When the wind fails or the tide turns foul you accept it and either do what you can or wait philosophically. If you do without an engine, you must buy an alarm clock, though, because you will be mustering to get under way at some very unsocial hours. There is neither night nor day, merely fair tide or foul.

Yet in busy waters I am nervous without an engine because things are then no longer in my own hands but in equal measure in the hands of others. To cross busy shipping lanes becomes a worrying nightmare. The pity is that I cannot be sufficiently strong-willed to use my engine solely in need instead of cranking it up to save a tide or because a failing wind means a dawn arrival on the mooring if I don't use it. There is no shame in motoring or motorsailing because it is merely a method of making a passage quickly and efficiently, but there is a lot of lost pleasure in it. I can't think of many sailing delights to equal that of feeling the first faint stir of a returning breeze just as you had become reconciled to another night out.

Any cruising or offshore racing yachtsman knows what happens to his dead (deduced?) reckoning once he begins riding a fast tidal current. You must know exactly where you are before you get into its clutches and you must also know exactly where you intend to go. Pathfinding your way along a labyrinthine rock-flanked channel in fast tidal waters leaves you no margin for even momentary error. You may be able to see beacons and seamarks in plenty, but by the time you have taken a set of bearings and plotted them on the chart the first and the last bearings taken have opened up like a rook's nest. Ship's head by plotted compass course may also be suspect, partly because the swirls and swillies may make a good course hard to hold and partly, as in our case, because the tidal set may be other than you expect.

Provident

Long and calm study of chart and pilotbook well in advance of reaching the channel is essential. I began reading it up only shortly beforehand, having missed the Chanel du Four. By studying in advance, and that includes before sailing, the chart and the book become familiar ground when the time arrives. You can note a series of possible transits and then stand by the helm watching for them to swing into and out of line as you hurtle by. If the channel is new to you, it will certainly appear different from your mental picture of it but the marks as you find them will be old friends.

Before anchoring anywhere it is time well spent to make one or two passes over the chosen spot to size it up. You have to know where to place the anchor in order that the yacht, when brought up at the end of her scope, will lie where you had planned. If the anchorage is tight, it pays to have somebody else on the helm during these passes so that you can stand in the bows looking around. You can then better visualize just where the anchor must be let go. To try to judge this from aft at the helm means that you are a ship's length away when you order the anchor to be dropped – in the case of *Provident*, some eighty feet out.

Many years after my successful berthing under sail I was to sail a few times in the Thames sailing barge *Cambria* (skipper-owner the late 'Bob' Roberts), and to see what handling an engineless vessel was all about. Plying up south and down north, as the bargemen say, referring to the ebb and flood tides, between Great Yarmouth and London Docks both summer and winter, Bob had to know what steerage way the barge would carry according to her cargo. Loading a heavy cargo like cement in sacks was very different matter from taking aboard a cargo of bulky though lighter goods and she would shoot differently.

I remember waiting one winter night for *Cambria* to arrive at West India Dock. I waited in the PLA offices on the quay by the open lock gates, for Bob was due up on top of the flood so that he could sail straight in. He was late. The PLA lock keeper and his assistant knew nothing about sailing vessels and I had to reassure them that having a dead beat up river for much of the way would delay Bob a bit. Suddenly we saw her out in the river, driving hard in the rainy, squally night. We saw her luff up and her headsail come down and her mainsail melt away as it was brailed up, then her bows came to starboard and she came bald-head at the lock entrance. 'He's going to pile 'er up!' moaned the PLA man. In she came, navigation oil lamps winking, bow-wave slapping and her rigging soughing aloft.

She passed into the patch of light from the dockside and we saw that there was nobody on the wheel, yet still she came. The PLA men rushed out of their hut yelling and waving. Then I saw Bob. He was standing at the bulwarks calmly peeing over the side. 'That you up there, Des?' he called out.

The barge carried her way right through the locks and right across the huge span of the dock into the berth nominated for her where the mate stepped easily ashore with his lines.

Reefing bowsprits were an essential part of a working trawler's gear. Instead of being fixed, the bowsprit could be run in, having a heelrope to control it and to run it out again later. An iron fid secured it in place. The bowsprit could be run in out of the way in dock and shortened (reefed) in bad weather at sea, but it is said that on some occasions it was also used as a buffer when sailing into a harbour berth. There were no steam tugs at Brixham and trawlers usually came up to moorings for unloading, but sometimes they must have had to bring up in the dock. The late Jock Beardson, a fellow ICC skipper of the lovely ex-trawler *Rulewater*, also then owned by the club and sadly long since rotted beyond repair, once shot a berth in this fashion.

The yachtsmen who originally converted *Provident* not only fixed her bowsprit but built a foc'sle companionway slap in the way of its heel so that it never could be run in, but *Rulewater* still had her reefing 'sprit. Jock, a laconic man and a superb seaman under sail, luffed her straight for the entrance and, having passed inside, turned her hard to starboard into the berth. He had the fid out of the bowsprit and a good hand on the heelrope. As she ran into her berth the end of the bowsprit met the wall, so I'm told, and the heelrope was surged away handsomely to bring her up smoothly and gently. Jock was forbidden ever to try it again.

Little more needs to be said about umbrella warping. It is unlikely that any yachtsman will have to try it in a modern yacht of average size. In the event that it is tried, though, it is the person who is handling the dinghy under oars who makes or ruins the operation. He must be able to spin, stop and ship oars, lodge the kedge, then pull away fast to keep ahead of the ship and to get far enough ahead to place his anchor – again, smartly. He has to do this not once, but again and again and again.

11

Collision

It was a dark night but clear, the moon was down and cloud hid the stars. At sea level, though, visibility was good and distant lights were diamond-sharp as we closed on Salcombe from about twelve miles to the south. We were making for home after a two-week cruise along the North Brittany coast, sailing about four knots in the moderate easterly breeze. It was eleven o'clock at night and I was thinking about Salcombe bar and whether we would be getting inshore too soon for crossing, debating whether to lie off or to anchor in the Range where there would be shelter unless a swell was running in.

There wasn't a lot of shipping about. I could see a couple of ships to the westward shaping to pass inward bound to seaward of us and there was another distant vessel also to seaward passing safely outward bound. Right inshore, though, I could see the lights of a fairly large ship off Start Point and heading west. I wondered why she was so close inshore and supposed that she was going to make her number to the watch on Prawle Point which flanks Salcombe entrance to the east.

We dipped on our way over a gentle swell. It was all very peaceful. The binnacle light shone upwards over the helmsman's face as he concentrated on his job. At the end of a cruise even the rawest beginners could hold a good course, especially in such easy conditions, and I was watching the inshore vessel just for something to do. After a short while I saw her lights swing and change from red to red-green and then green and I wondered at such a sharp change of course, but she was all of eight miles away and now heading clear to the eastward. After only a few minutes, to my surprise, she turned and resumed her original course. 'He's playing silly b———s,' one of my watch said. I agreed and guessed he'd put in a short leg to get further offshore, but it was odd.

It must have been ten or twelve minutes later, when the ship was by then off Salcombe and we were about three-quarters of a mile further on, that she did exactly the same thing again, although this time she showed us both red and green and masthead whites in line as she headed directly offshore and towards us. The distance between us was, perhaps, five miles. I became alert. In those pre-Radar reflector days our modest navigation lights might have been visible at three miles and being under sail we had no white steaming light. As a routine precaution I found and rigged the Aldis light and then resumed my watch. I switched on the light and held a steady beam towards her for a minute. Gradually she turned and gave us her safe green.

In hindsight such erratic behaviour should have made me more suspicious than I was and I should have started our engine and held it at tick-over, but this would have meant quitting the deck for some minutes, because it wasn't an easy engine to start. I preferred to remain where I was, and I wasn't going to trust anybody else messing with the prima donna of an engine. Anyway, the ship was now steady and on present showing she should pass on a reciprocal course about a quarter of a mile to the east of us. She should pass quite safely provided neither she nor we altered toward the other. The minutes passed as we continued on our way at our easy, swinging four knots with the booms well squared off and the headsails giving an occasional flap. 'Just keep her going steady,' I told the helmsman, 'and don't let her swing towards him at all or you'll show your port and starboard together and confuse him.'

There was perhaps a mile between us, then less, and the gap was closing with that curious rapidity which is an illusion of the sea, when two vessels seem to rush together after a long period of seeming suspension. Suddenly the other ship took form and became audible and it was plain that she would pass starboard to starboard at a good deal less than a quarter of a mile, but safely still if she held course. I gave her a steady Aldis beam which I held and then panned up over our sails and back again. It seemed simultaneous with my signal that she suddenly began turning *directly towards us*.

Recollections thereafter are confused. I remember grabbing the wheel and holding the rim spoke, pumping it over to leeward as fast as I could. My instinct and long familiarity with *Hoshi* told me not to try tacking. She would turn faster downwind. Why turn anyway? I didn't have time to think; only to bear off and reduce our length.

We were all yelling our heads off. I have a vision of the ship coming at us in huge bounds with the thunder of her bow wave and the

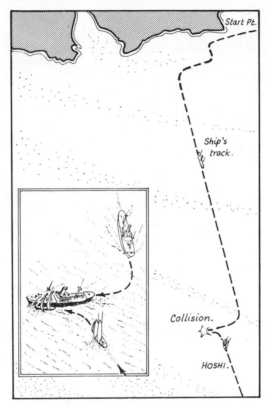

Collision in the English Channel.

metallic thud of her engines. She seemed to be growing up into the sky into a black, light-studded tower that loomed over us as we slowly turned our seventy-foot length away from her, presenting our stern. I remember slamming and slamming the rudder against its stops as if I thought to get more and more helm on her.

She came down on us like a huge black axe. What I recall now is a last-minute sense of strange and unreal detachment, as if I were watching all this happen to somebody else. I felt no fear at all, just this odd sensation of floating detachment. Joyce rose from her bunk in the sail locker at our feet, she was clutching her cat. Those who had been below came tumbling up the companionway having heard our shouting. The axe was going to cut us in half!

We were still turning away – almost too late – then a rolling, roaring twelve-foot wall of water hit us and thrust us aside, burying our decks, heeling us. . . . Along our side went the ship with row upon row of steel plates grinding our rail, ripping up stanchions, tearing out davits, while from aloft fell spars and wires and ropes. There was a deafening drumming of propeller wake and she was past. We were still alive.

I found that I was shaking from head to foot. Everybody was rushing around and talking loudly, asking what had happened, grabbing my arm. I began to give orders of some sort, but I was totally disorientated. A woman was screaming that we were sinking; that water was rushing into the cabin. Joyce was at the time five months pregnant with our daughter and Judy Russell (later to skipper *Hoshi* for many years) was sailing as mate. They began to assemble people on deck and see that all had their lifejackets. I remember a girl who was a chain-smoker suddenly trying to fight her way below again for her cigarettes and a man sitting numb with fright. I battled my way below and forced myself to conduct a calm inspection of the whole of our starboard side, listening for water rushing in but not hearing it, trying to believe our luck. Judy was working the deck pump and I heard it sucking dry in the pump well.

Back on deck, I saw that we were lying half-lead to wind with sails slatting and that the ship which had hit us was lying stopped half a mile downwind. I got the sheets freed. The main gaff was broken in half and the starboard crosstree was gone. We bore off towards the ship while I got the engine started.

We came up with her and passed along her starboard side towards her stern where people were standing in the light of deck lamps. Someone asked if we were all right; were we going to sink? 'What ship are you?' I called. Nobody replied and I asked again, then a third time, 'What ship are you?' Then I saw a portly man in pyjamas running towards the stern. He cupped his hands and gave me the name of the ship and asked the name of our yacht and were we all right?

They stood by us while I made another inspection below and then, upon my assurance that we could make Salcombe unaided, we parted company and we began to motor towards home. Twice during the remainder of our passage shorewards two other ships deviated and closed on us, shining their searchlights to check our safety, no doubt in response to a radio all-ships message. The sight of these ships bearing down on us was terrifying.

I have not included the name of the ship which hit us because the insurance matter was settled out of court in our favour. The name is irrelevant. Suffice to say that she was thirteen thousand tons, bound for Canada and carrying mail. How she came to run us down I heard very much later.

It seems that a fourth mate had the watch. Upon finding the ship drawing too close to land, he ordered a big course alteration only to discover after a minute or so that this brought him on a collision course with the outward-bound ships to which I referred earlier. Accordingly, he altered back – again a ninety-degree alteration – and found to his mounting panic that he was now on a collison course with one of the *inward*-bound vessels. Again he altered offshore. The final alteration – almost fatal for us – came when he found that the second of the two inward-bound ships was now on a converging course. At no time did he ask for or heed advice. If anybody saw our Aldis and reported it to him, the report must have been ignored.

Conclusions

There may not be many collisions reported between yachts and ships, but there must be countless near-collisions and the number rises as both types of traffic increase. A great deal is written on the subject of collision avoidance, on the Rules of the Road at Sea, the Separation Zone systems and so forth. A lot of it gets forgotten.

There is a curious blind spot, though, which pictures the big ship as a form of obstruction proceeding steadily and *quite mechanically* along her course, to be given the right of way in some instances and expected to give way, mechanically, in others. The possibility of rogue ships is agreed, also ships with flag-of-convenience crews which may do odd things at times. The sheer size of the big ship implies a standard of professional conduct far above that of which yachtsmen might be capable; in most cases this standard is upheld. It is equally true that human beings, with all their frailties, angers, prides, stupidities and physical weaknesses, order the behaviour of all ships.

This is the paramount factor to consider. Having taken all steps to avoid collision and having seen that the danger is apparently past, we must still remember the unseen human being with the toothache or the stubborn battle of wills that may be taking place on the bridge.

Collisions don't just happen. There is stage 1, a state of convergence or course changes leading to collision (such as when a big ship changes course because her draft compels her); and there is stage 2, actual *avoidance* of collision when a split-second helm movement one way or the other can decide the fate of the yacht. Stage 1 is a matter of seafaring education and I haven't space to deal with the many aspects of it here. Stage 2 is another matter. Like any last-second emergency, be it fire, man overboard or anything else of that nature, it is less a *thinking* situation than an instinctive one. Placed in such a position, a person is likely to freeze:

It was lucky that I did the right thing. On the other hand, it was the right thing only because we survived. Was it the *best* thing? The thought has haunted me ever since. Suppose we had stood on, not borne away at all? Might we not have just cleared her bows with our stern, comfortably cleared them perhaps? As it was, we were pushed aside by the bow wave just enough for the ship to fall alongside us, and nowadays, had the ship been one with a bulbous bow, we would probably have been rolled over and down in a matter of seconds.

In those last seconds a helmsman may have to decide this very question of stand on or turn to reduce the size of target by presenting a yacht's bow or stern. One important factor prevents an easy decision. Ships at sea may seem to be proceeding in a dead-straight line, but in fact they are often swinging a few degrees from port to starboard and back as the helmsman, or autopilot, corrects the helm, and the viewer dead ahead who makes a decision to open up the engine and go straight ahead may be absolutely wrong.

I bore away because it was the only turning option. Bearing away must win a few seconds of time, just as turning towards the ship must surrender a few seconds. On the other hand, a small yacht taking a very near miss and being confronted by a bow wave, or a glancing blow even, might be better able to take it forward than by the cockpit.

Some steps are obvious sense, such as trying to decide that danger is building up and that crew ought to be roused out from below and wearing lifejackets. Obvious sense, perhaps, but what skipper is going to put the fear of God into a timid crew when he still isn't all that certain of the existence of danger? In shipping and thick fog the danger is all too obvious to need stressing, but in clear weather a chance encounter with a big ship that doesn't seem to be willing to alter course for a yacht under sail is far less obvious.

Many ships at sea today will *not* alter for a sailing yacht if the yachtsman can be scared into altering first. I once experienced this with a ship way out in the Atlantic some two hundred miles from land, in daylight and with no other vessels in sight. From first seeing her as a speck over the horizon we watched her come closer, on a collision course. We had the wind vane steering gear set and I didn't want to disengage it. I stood on and the ship stood on. It ended with us disengaging the gear very smartly, hauling the helm up, letting run the mainsail and carving close round the ship's stern. Her watch officer and crew gave us friendly waves and smiles.

Nowadays I am craven about shipping. I give way to all big ships, although unobtrusively so that confusion cannot arise, far in advance of a potential convergence. I either make a distinctive course alteration or slow down a little. The crossing of a separation lane is a different problem because in the southern North Sea where I sail there is often such a tight line of ships to cross that to slow for one means to fall foul of the next, but give way one must even if it means heaving to for a while outside the lane and waiting for a bigger gap. It is then that having a fairly powerful auxiliary engine is such a comfort, allowing one to get through at maximum hull speed. Perhaps it is sad to have to acknowledge once and for all that an engine must play such a vital role in the way of a sailing vessel. It need not, of course. You could still get by very nicely without an engine, but not safely if you sail in busy commercial waters.

Like all sudden emergencies, the main danger is focused on the split-second when the mind freezes and the body becomes momentarily numbed. Then comes the charge of adrenalin demanding action and whether the right action is taken depends upon luck and past experience. If the situation has arisen before, or been planned for and thought about, then there is a very good chance that the subconscious will come up with an order which will be the *right* one.

12

Man Overboard

The race had started in a full force 8 with a weather-going beat down the Solent and out through the Needles that had soaked us all to the bone and washed out the accommodation. None of us had a dry change left. The night that followed was a battle I shall never forget. Under deep-reefed main and storm jib, we clawed our way to the west until the meagre ground we covered for such awful effort convinced our owners that it would be better to lie hove-to for the remaining hours of darkness. The head-long crashes and the constant blast of flung spray, against which the helmsman had to stare, had left all of us blinded.

The early forecast spoke of yet more gales in the west. The wind decreased to force 6–7. The owners decided wisely that, with the shelter of Brixham Harbour lying within easy reach on the inshore tack, it would be no bad thing to invest in a few hours' rest, a good meal and perhaps dry out the bedding. It was full daylight, we were on a port-quartering run under small canvas and with a foreguy on the boom. As might be imagined, the sea was big and steering was fairly hard work.

I was alone on watch, at the wheel. The other four men were below, the watch having just changed, and some attempt at getting breakfast was being made. John, let us call him, came on deck to empty the gash bucket. He had on his oilskins and, I believe, his boots (although I don't recall for certain), and neither safety harness nor lifejacket. The event happened some twenty-five years ago and at that time neither was worn much – I'm not even sure that harnesses had been invented then.

He stood to leeward on the side deck, one hand on the coachroof grab rail, the other to deal with the bucket. Having dumped the contents, tins and all, in the random fashion of those times, he needed to swill it out, but with one hand he couldn't get it to fill. I saw his hand leave the grab rail just as a big sea lurched up under the port quarter. I yelled a warning, but it was too late. John seemed barely to touch the guardrail as he went head first over the side.

I yelled the chilling words at the top of my voice. Alan, one of the owners, was at my side in seconds. I let go of the wheel as he grabbed it. 'Watch him,' he said.

The rest of the crew tumbled up from below. There was much to be done. Until the foreguy was let go, we could not manoeuvre. John fell astern, visible by virtue of his yellow oilies. He was visible less and less frequently, though, and soon there was only a very occasional glimpse of him on a wave crest.

The manoeuvres, the handling of the yacht, were superb. Handling the yacht is only a small part of the operation, however, and if we had lost John, as we nearly did, the blame would have been laid squarely upon the inadequacy of the equipment of those days and on our crewing. There are several versions of what actually happened and some are slightly at variance with mine. I can only tell it as I remember it.

Alan brought us up and stopped us within feet of John. Someone threw the first lifebuoy. In those days there were a good many canvas, kapok-filled buoys to be found and this was one. It had become absolutely saturated. It simply sank.

We went round again, bore off, gybed and again Alan came close. This time a new buoy was produced, but it was so light and buoyant that it went skimming downwind like a bird, with no hope of John catching hold of it. Round we went again, and on this occasion a heaving line was tried. It was neatly done up in a buntline hitch, but so tightly that by the time it was undone and hastily thrown it was a mess of tangles that fell woefully short. I have a recollection that a third lifebuoy had been thrown, this one with a line on it that was secured to the after end of the pulpit and which by reason of that line had been torn out of John's grasp as the ship filled away and bore off. Perhaps this was another incident entirely, but it happened, and I have always doubted the wisdom of a buoy attached in that fashion.

By the time we were coming round yet again, it was almost too late. I shall never forget the sight of John's face, pale and distorted *under water*. Somebody, in sheer desperation, threw the tail of the jib sheet and, feeling it fall across his arm, some instinct made John grab it and hang on. Within seconds hands could reach down and grasp his clothing. Alan had given us a lee side or we would never have reached him; neither would we have reached him from the rail of many of today's high freeboard yachts. This should have been the end of the matter but it was only the beginning of the real struggle.

A lot of well-meaning lip service is paid to the theory of recovering a person from the water. People shake their heads and agree that it is indeed a difficult task – without ever (mercifully) having tried it for real. There was a time that awful day when three of us, all fit, strong men, had expended all the effort we were capable of making. The guardrails were not fitted with slips or lanyards for easy release, John's pockets and clothing were incredibly heavy with water and he was a big man. I believe it must have been ten or more minutes before we got him halfway through the rails.

Conclusions

In my view there is almost too much consideration given to the pick-up *manoeuvre* in books and in instruction. I don't suggest that it is of less importance than other aspects, but I think that the division of schools of thought into 'gybe first' or 'don't gybe', 'start the engine', or 'reach off and back' is a bit of a red herring. What is of absolute importance is that it should have been thought about and thought about constantly; day or night an owner and his leading hands should speculate while sailing – if it happened, now, what would I do?

The 'reach-off-and-then-reach-back' method increases the chances of finding the person. It puts the boat under good control for regulating speed and it buys time during which the crew can be organized. A gybe has to be almost instantaneous if it is to bring the boat back to the person in the water – which in any case would probably find the crew still not ready to deal with things. A heavy gybe could even cause damage or injury. And yet there may well be occasions when a gybe would suit the circumstances.

Perhaps the only real benefit of having a rigidly laid-down drill is that it is instinctive. It takes over while the crew are still dazed by what has happened. It is possible for a skipper to be numb with shock and to react by giving a stream of orders resulting in a heightening of panic and chaos on deck. This problem of shocked disbelief is crucial. It happens again and again.

In our case the man who took charge not only stayed calm but he also made the right decisions in the right *order*. In a case of man overboard a lot of orders may need to be given; imagine getting them out of proper sequence. Alan said, 'Watch him'. Suppose he had sent me to the foreguy and yelled for someone to attend the lifebuoys, another to attend to the jib sheets. All proper orders, but suppose the instruction to watch the man in the water had been delayed and John had been wearing a navy sweater instead of yellow oilskins? Nowadays in a well-equipped yacht he might have shouted the one word 'Danbuoy', or my first action upon raising the alarm would have been to trigger the release mechanism of a flagbuoy, a danbuoy. This mark-at-once drill is probably the most important of all and if it is instinctive in everybody it will probably give a lost person a greatly heightened chance of survival.

He will see that something has been done and take heart. If possible he will make for the buoy and get support from it. Then the crew can concentrate on handling the ship. In rough water it is particularly important and at night vitally so. A danbuoy with its tall staff, light and flag, is vastly superior to floating lights of any sort, which at best are seen only occasionally as they lift on the wave crests. At night such a flagstaff, with retro-reflective tape on it, can be picked up brilliantly at the full range of the strongest duty torch aboard and this tape may be more reliable than a light on the staff.

No proper drill can be right for all occasions, only partly right; very right for some and inadequate for others. The rescuers have to think. A man known as a strong swimmer and a strong character, provided he was not knocked on the head in falling, is going to stay afloat by his own efforts and do the things expected of him; in this case the crew may have more time to be painstaking. A known poor swimmer, a panicky person, or anyone over the side when seas are winter-cold, needs instant help. It is my belief that the first action then should be to turn the boat as fast as possible and sail so close to the person that a lifebuoy can be pushed into his hands, buying time. Somebody should shout encouragement to him. Panic kills and encouragement is its antidote.

In the preceding story, much of what went wrong was because of lack of proper equipment and preparation – it was no fault of the owners. It was normal for the times to have the sort of gear that we had – guardrails that couldn't be let go in an emergency, a hemp heaving line that knotted and tangled, and no particular regard for life harnesses. Nowadays things are very different, particularly in the offshore racing fleets, and I think we would have been better able to cope. But certain features remain as much a risk as ever and one of them is recovery of a heavy person from the water.

Many people conscientiously practise what they call man-overboard drills. They chuck a lifebuoy over and bring her to a stop close by. The buoy is then recovered with the boathook. This manoeuvre is as much like the real thing as a fire drill without fire and in which the use of fire extinguishers is mimed. It serves some purpose, but it is no preparation for what really happens.

The person overboard may be capable of only one all-out effort to help himself struggle up the side and those trying to haul him up are similarly handicapped. Leaning over a rail from a cockpit places the body at a disadvantage. There is no purchase for the feet and the distance outwards involves lying painfully across the coaming. From further forward on the side deck there is no option but to kneel with a shoulder wedged against a stanchion. Further forward still by the main shrouds there may be the increased height of the topsides. Add the rolling of the yacht and you get a situation in which nobody can exert more than a fraction of their full strength in a lift. One all-out effort and thereafter, unless some mechanical aid to climbing is used, the odds against complete rescue rise fast. People have been brought alongside and then lost because they could not be hauled aboard.

A strop, or a rope's end, must be got around the person in the water, round his back below his armpits, and tied with a knot on his chest. Unless you know how to make a bowline from upside down and can make it without thinking it shouldn't be attempted. Most people in this sort of urgency will make two half-hitches. This will mean that any attempt to lift by the rope will cause the loop to tighten painfully, but at least he will be secure for a while, buying more time.

It is imperative that a lee side is presented to the man. For this reason, leaving the sails set will help because once the man is grasped the yacht can be laid hove-to with headsail aback, mainsail hardened in and tiller lashed to leeward. The angle of heel plus the weight of crew will hold the rail well down.

A boarding ladder is usually advocated but a lot depends upon its type. The sort which hooks over the toerail is secure unless it is kicked sideways, when it will unhook and go overboard, and a sideways kick is exactly what is likely to happen. A ladder of this design must have a rope sling in addition which is of a length to drop over a handy winch or cleat on the coaming, thus allowing the ladder to be lowered down so that the bottom step is a foot or more below the surface of the water. A rope ladder is useless. Lying flat against the hull, or washing far under the turn of the bilge as the yacht drifts to leeward, perhaps hove-to, it is unlikely that a struggling person's feet could find it. Any rope ladder must have either steps or spacers to hold it clear. The old idea of forming a rope bight or loop down into the water to act as a foot step has a lot of merit, but one end should be turned up on a sheet winch to offer the option of shortening it up by degrees – perhaps with each roll down of the yacht. Permanent ladders on the stern are sometimes well placed and in other cases very badly placed because the man has to be handed round to the stern, with the after pulpit obstructing the rescuers. If the yacht is pitching, the ladder will be rising and falling violently and, if the stern is an outward-raking transom, the person in the water will have to climb at a difficult angle. With the engine running in neutral there may be an additional danger and it is as well to say that if the engine has been started to aid manoeuvres it should be shut off completely the moment the person has been grasped alongside.

There are a number of recommended ways of recovering a person from overboard, including the use of the boom and mainsheet or topping lift on a mast winch as a derrick. The mainsail is run out of its track and overboard so that the body can be cradled in it and raised by the main halyard. Or the headsail can be lowered over the side, secured along its luff to the toerail and the man rolled up by hauling or winching on the clew. All these methods demand a high standard of seamanship and plenty of helpers. In a wind and sea of any weight they would be very difficult and time-consuming. They might work, and indeed some *have* worked, but much depends upon size of yacht and winch power, and they might constitute a tragic waste of valuable time.

There is one other method. Many people like to carry a half-inflated dinghy on deck while on passage. In this condition it resembles a big horseshoe with a floor in it. Launched overboard, open end towards the man, it provides a small, safe 'dock' into which he can be dragged and held pending final lifting.

We have so far assumed that the yacht has a crew on deck of at least three grown men and this is the most dangerous assumption of the lot. A huge percentage of yachts at sea are family-crewed by parents and half-grown children, or even young children. Since it is father who usually does the deck work, he is the most vulnerable to going overboard.

There are two plain essentials. The wife must be able to manoeuvre under sail or engine well enough to turn and stop the boat close by and there must be very careful thought and attention given to equipment, beginning with harness-wearing and including danbuoy drill and means of boarding from the water. It is not sufficient to be able to start and operate the engine. In any weight of wind, under sail, the headsail will louse up any manoeuvre. So she must also be capable, singlehanded, of dropping and roughly securing at least the headsail. The mainsail left up will steady the yacht, provided she avoids downwind attitudes. It all calls for personal practice in advance.

The equipment I have available when sailing as half of a husband-and-wife team consists of a danbuoy, a quick-release lifebuoy with its drogue and light and a twenty-metre floating line with a quoit at the end. My guardrails are on slips and a boarding ladder hangs permanently ready for use on the after pulpit. My wife (in the event of my unscheduled plunge) would (a) pull the release handle; (b) collect her wits and turn the boat back; and (c) grab the second lifebuoy from the hatch stowage and thrust it into my hands as she went close by. She would have bought time. According to the conditions she would then have to decide whether to drop sail and motor or to sail past, trailing the floating line into my grasp, and then just let fly sheets completely so that the yacht gradually stopped. If she wanted to lower the headsail she would also stop the boat in this way and the boat, as we have found by experiment, would lie roughly beam-on and scarcely moving. Once alongside she would drop guardrails and hang out the boarding ladder. Provided I had not been left too long in the cold sea and I had not been injured in my fall, I am confident I would be able to get aboard. If I was incapable of doing so, I would be as good as dead, because with high topsides and a lone woman to raise a wet, soaked, limp and heavy man there would be no way of her overcoming the problem without immediate outside help.

The dangerous incident described in the first part of this chapter occurred in broad daylight. I have no doubt that had it been under similar conditions at night we would have lost John. There is a lot of difference. Crew roused from below at night come up totally disorientated. If the yacht is gybed, even the watch on deck will be disorientated at first, particularly on a very dark night. There is only one thing that is going to save a man overboard and that is a lighted buoy in the water or at least a retro-reflective one. Human sense of direction is unreliable and doing mental sums in order to steer a reciprocal course back to the person invites error.

If I were briefly to sum up the proper technique for rescue – and I haven't by any means dealt exhaustively with the subject here – I think I would do so in two words: *Danbuoy, ladder*. If we can be sure that the first and instinctive reaction to man overboard, by day or by night, is to let go a lighted buoy *instantly*, we would go a very long way to coping with this terrible emergency. In our case, if we had had a proper ladder we would not have come so close to tragedy.

13

The Instinct

There is usually a funny side to any sailing adventure, but not this one. We narrowly missed certain destruction and even now, a quarter of a century later, I shudder at our close escape.

It happened during a Lyme Bay race and I was a last-minute crewman, a pierhead jumper, in a middle-of-the-fleet yacht entered for this early-season race. The Lyme Bay race no longer exists since the lone buoy in the middle of the bay was removed, thereby doing away with one of the most exasperating turning marks that Channel offshore racing has ever seen.

We started from Southsea on a drizzly, cold Friday evening with a south-westerly almost dead on the nose for our first mark, which was the CH 1 buoy outside Cherbourg, and the watches that night were comfortless. We seemed to be doing well, though, but it called for great effort and vigilance both to race the boat and to watch for tacking yachts and big shipping in the poor visibility. The owner drove himself hard, taking no rest at all.

We rounded in early daylight and began broad reaching back across channel for the Lyme Bay buoy. It was a terrific sail. The weather brightened and we drove the yacht at her maximum hull speed for hours on end. The owner cat-napped a little but still took no proper rest. We were up with the front runners in our class and he was exultant and anxious by turns. By late afternoon we were approaching the middle of Lyme Bay, the sun had disappeared and the wind was westerly rising and bringing a belt of thin, cold rain.

Finding the buoy was what this race was all about. RDF was less sophisticated then, and while one could get good beam bearings it was less easy to find a good cross. In theory the plan was to find and follow a line of soundings, combining this method with RDF and DR in the hope of finding that lonely buoy which worked fairly well in good visibility but made it pure gamble in poor. The Rules allowed for this problem, however, and the buoy could be rounded unseen provided evidence of chart and workings could be produced along with the signatures of crew. After a bit of hunting around, our owner declared the buoy to have been rounded. We came on a dead run for home.

Plainly we were in for a windy night. We were on the port gybe with a poled-out genoa in lieu of a spinnaker and going as fast as the yacht could be driven. The owner was fretful at having failed to find the buoy, but determined now to put in a good time on the last leg and, being very tired, he was irritable and nervy. In due course we saw Portland light hazy in the driving rain and perhaps six or seven miles to port. It was very black, blowing about force 7, and there was a big and breaking following sea to make steering heavy. I came on watch with my co-watchkeeper at midnight when the Portland light was on the quarter.

We were doing four-hour watches and changing helmsmen frequently, due to the physical effort of steering. With the main boom out to starboard and the steepness of the following seas, the yacht was difficult to hold straight. Again and again we would start a broach to port, jamming on full rudder, letting the wheel spin back, catch and hold, then heaving it over again, while the wave crests divided and roared past us as she drove her bows deep. After two hours of this my mate began to get worried 'We're going much too fast,' he said, 'and we're sheering inshore all the time.'

I had been feeling the same thing. Every time we began a broach we were coming off course to port, towards the distant Dorset coast. This wasn't important but we both knew that our ordered course was to take us close past St Catherine's Point, south of the Wight. Both of us sailed those waters a lot. You get a feeling of position. It can be false but it can also be deadly accurate. I agreed with my mate's opinion and I suggested that since we couldn't even out our off-course swings we'd have to go on the other gybe sooner or later.

The owner stuck his head up shortly afterwards and we told him of our worries. 'You steer and I'll navigate, OK?' was all he said. The hours went by. As we broached to port again and again, griping up off our course, making more and more northing, we both became more and more uneasy. It is one thing to be able to go and look at the chart and plot an average course made good – to see for yourself – and another to sit for hour after hour in the roaring blackness trying to hold a course that you know to be suspect. We discussed it. 'I'll have another go at him,' I said. I stuck my head down the hatch.

'Sorry,' I hedged, 'but honestly we're not holding the course. We both feel we've let her stray miles out to the north of it. Do you think we should gybe her?' His face in the half-light of the chart table spotlight looked lined with exhaustion. 'I've allowed for all that. Just keep her going and keep your eyes open for St Catherine's light – that's your job.'

I reported back to my mate. 'I don't like it,' he worried, 'he hasn't allowed for it. We're still on the same heading we started with.' We changed places at the wheel. The run went on and on, now and then the genoa would give a slam that shook the whole boat; the wild surges continued and I grunted with effort as I inched the rockhard wheel over and back, over and back. I saw him go to the hatch and speak down it, then draw back as the owner thrust his head out.

'Gybe the bloody boat then!' he shouted at us. 'If you want to throw the race away and sail halfway out across the Channel then go ahead and gybe her, I'm finished.' He withdrew and to our astonishment he went to his quarter-berth and turned in, face hidden. We roused out hands and took in the pole, took off the boom foreguy and gybed her with a slam that put the yacht on her beam ends. The mate of the other watch noted time and log and laid off the new heading from the last DR position. He tried for an RDF bearing but we couldn't hold her steady enough to give him an 'on' (there were no hand-held instruments in those days). Then we were left to finish the last half-hour of our watch in the blackness that precedes the coming dawn.

It was perhaps ten minutes before we saw the light of St Catherine's Point. *It was on the wrong bow.* The light should have been wide on our port bow but it was instead small on our *starboard* bow. Quite plainly, prior to gybing, we had been shaping not to clear the Wight but straight into that graveyard of ships, the Atherfield Ledge on the south-western coast of the island.

We hauled our wind and laid up for a safe offing, holding St Catherine's light half a mile to port until we could bear off to a reach and weather the headland.

Conclusions

Physical and mental exhaustion is one of the biggest causes of loss of both ships and aircraft. There comes a time when an exhausted person ceases to be able to think and act normally. Mistakes are made, errors in navigation and errors of judgement, and false

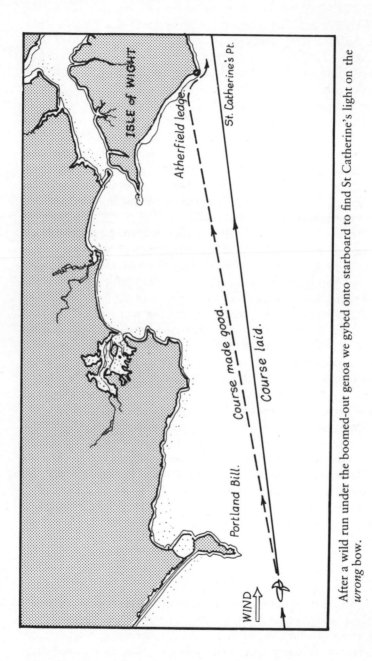

After a wild run under the boomed-out genoa we gybed onto starboard to find St Catherine's light on the *wrong* bow.

conclusions drawn. With it, too, come personality changes when the person allows petty feelings to take charge.

Our owner was a good and competent seaman and navigator. Most probably he had put in a hard day's work before driving to the coast for the start of the race. Thereafter he had driven himself to and beyond his limits. I have been most careful to avoid any clues to his or the yacht's identity because even now I don't blame him for what nearly happened.

It has happened to me. It can happen to any skipper. Our hunch that something was badly wrong was lucky, but no more than that. Hunches can be reliable, but they can also be equally dangerous unless they are a sort of gut-reaction based upon a full knowledge of all factors.

14

Beam Ends

Orari was a strip-planked twenty-four-footer, a Caravel class, just a bit tender with her heavy wooden mast, but a delight to handle. I was coming home singlehanded from around the coast and with about twelve miles to go into the Thames Estuary when the wind fell to a flat, glassy calm. In an hour's time the tide would go foul; not only that, but my drying mooring off Leigh would become a bit of rusty chain sitting in the sunshine on a vast desert of popping, hissing mud.

It was a very hot, humid afternoon with big thunderheads building up over the land. I had my big lightweight ghoster set and sheeted fairly close, but the last of my steerage way had dwindled to nothing. 'I will have to start the engine,' I told myself, much as Hannibal might have contemplated the crossing of the Alps.

It was a four-horse two-stroke about the size of a garden gnome, and it was no surprise that I swung its little handle in vain. I didn't waste long at that exercise either, but quickly followed it with plug changing, then spark testing and a look at the float chamber. I moved on into phase 2. I pencilled the plug points (a device that is supposed to produce a temporarily fat spark and reward the scribe with a bellow of unleased power). My pencil broke – every time I sharpened it it broke: it was one of those. I launched into the final cure. Lighting the cooker and using pliers, I held the plug points in the flame. Why I did this I can't say, but perhaps it has some pre-Christian significance.

I was standing there below, holding my offering to the flame when I heard what I thought to be a huge flock of birds in flight: the combined rush of a thousand wings, a deep, rushing sigh . . . The next moment the yacht was flat on her ear with her rudder completely out of water, her lee sheet winch deeply immersed and water pouring solidly in a cataract through the open companionway.

I struggled out waist-deep and locked my arms around the oppo-

104

site sheet winch level with my chin. I recovered my marbles and began groping underwater for the ghoster sheet to let it go, but I couldn't find it. The mainsheet jammed after a couple of feet had run free. The thunder squall held us there, pinned flat, sinking by the second, while the sea smoked with blown spume. Then, just as suddenly as it had arrived, the squall passed. It left a fresh force 5 in its wake and a very wet, frightened and cursing Sleightholme.

With water below almost level with the bunk tops, too much sail on her and, with a dramatic shift of wind direction, a lee shore no more than a mile away, I became a very busy man.

Conclusions

Unreliable engines are always bad news and this one was the cause of my being below. On the other hand, I might simply have gone below to look at the chart or brew some tea. My main error lay in not reading the weather and in particular the cloud that caused the squall because it was there to see.

Thunder squalls are almost always violent and arrive with surprising speed. Had I been on deck I would have seen a blackening line advancing ahead of a haze of rain. Mercifully such squalls seldom last for long, but long enough to overpower, dismast, rip sails and possibly drive a yacht ashore. In similar circumstances today I would be popping my head in and out of the hatch as if I were at a turkey shoot – an unhappily apt description, having regard for the wreckage for the years.

I didn't have a knife handy. This is incredible, because I would as soon venture forth in my bloomers as do so without a knife of some sort. For many years I was a sheath-knife man – that was in big gaff-rigged yachts. I wore a Breton fisherman's gutting knife in a homemade sheath and I used it constantly, but with my change to quite tiny boats this Excalibur looked silly. Perhaps my knife was in a jacket pocket – a jacket taken off because the day was so hot? If I had had a knife I would have slashed the underwater sheet without hesitation, thus letting the poor little ship stagger to her feet.

If she had been held there until she sank under me, what then? I had no dinghy except a vast and ancient deflated inflatable stuffed deep down in the forepeak and out of reach. There was no lifejacket. A lifebuoy on the stern was all I would have had – provided I could reach it.

Distress signals? They were below and there is no guarantee that a swimmer in a blast of rain could fire them off – in any case, with what result? Could I have swum ashore? Perhaps I could have covered that mile – if I knew in which direction the shore lay (which I didn't in that blinding rain) – but the following force 5 sea would have made it a poor gamble.

15

Look Daddy, They're Waving

Cygnet was a little four-ton gaff cutter, old but cherished, a nice little sailer but once again with an untrustworthy auxiliary. It was an old Morris car engine converted to marine use by a maniac, a mad, horrific engine, yet not directly to blame for this incident.

In a sense it was the cause of my error, for so obsessed was I with the need to pamper and wait upon this machine, to humour it and placate it, that I wasn't navigating properly. That engine, just to give an idea, had a crash gearbox and the handle went aft for ahead, forward for aft with a terrible clashing and grinding, but that was the least of it. There was a water priming cock which had to be closed the moment that a jet of rusty water shot upwards upon starting the engine. The throttle was a threaded rod with a knurled nut on it; if in a hurry, you had to open or close the throttle by first baring one forearm and then spinning the nut against your arm with an energetic series of elbow jerks which looked odd through binoculars.

Joyce and I with our small daughter came out of Ramsgate bound for Calais outside the Goodwins. The wind was easterly or thereabouts and we had a fresh beat out round the North Goodwin Lightvessel in that truly horrible lump of sea which the North Foreland seems to breed. By the time we had rounded it and borne off on a reach against the foul north-going tide, we had had enough. Almost at once the wind began to ease and I had a feeling that soon the engine would be needed.

It had behaved itself while leaving harbour, but like many a husband who detects in his wife a certain note of voice, a certain crispness of speech, he knows that trouble is not far away – just what he has done wrong he isn't certain, but sure as hell he mustn't put a foot out of place! The engine had had that feel about it and, like the cautious husband who fills the coal scuttle without being asked, and looks as though he's enjoying it, I felt it was time to clean the fuel filter and look at the plugs.

The East Goodwin Lightvessel lay some miles ahead on the bow. We were well outside the sands, far further outside than we needed to be, but I was being very careful. 'Now, then,' I told Joyce, 'keep the East Goodwin just open on your port bow. I want to go just inside it to keep out of the shipping.' She settled down to steer with Michele by her side towing her plastic pottie on a string as usual. I went below and began messing about with the spanners.

We dropped speed gradually as the wind eased but we were still making over the tide. The engine was proving unusually difficult to dismantle. I had all my spanners out, but they were primitive. Like most people I kept my good tools at home and took rubbish to sea for dealing with the real emergencies and my spanners were sheer archaeology. I finally unscrewed the problem nut by wedging the blade of a screwdriver into the gap between the spanner flats and petrol dripped into the tin can arranged below. 'Daddy,' my small daughter called, 'some fishermen are waving to us.' 'That's nice,' I said absently, 'wave back to them.'

A few minutes passed. 'How are we doing?' I asked up through the hatch. I had reached the tricky bit where the float chamber, having been cleaned of muck, won't seat itself properly on its gasket when you try to put it back. 'How are we doing? I repeated. Joyce wasn't altogether happy. 'I'm still aiming to keep the lightship just on our port bow, but the wind's coming ahead a little bit and it's getting rougher.' I could feel the boat jerking around.

'They're still waving, Daddy,' Michèle said, 'both arms too.' Suddenly I felt a stab of unease and, leaving the engine, I climbed out into the cockpit. Right away I saw that things were badly wrong. Joyce was still holding the course I had given her but she was looking alarmed and I saw why. All around us the sea was beginning to jerk itself into little pyramidal waves. To seaward in a fishing boat two men were anchored far distant, but waving their arms in great agitation. I took the helm and turned *Cygnet* up into the wind and right round until she was closehauled on starboard, sailing straight out to seawards away from the Goodwins. I guessed what was wrong with a sense of deep guilt for my own absolute stupidity in committing one of the basic nagivational sins. Instead of giving Joyce just a target to aim for I should have given her a compass course as well, then, when we began to sheer bodily towards the Goodwins, she would have known that something was wrong. Even though her bows were firmly on target the *attitude* of the boat was altering.

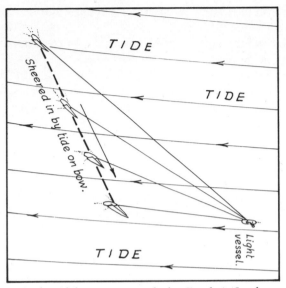

Set by tidal stream towards the Goodwin Sands.

Conclusions

Once at sea there is no time during which a skipper can get off the pot. Even when everything seems to be going well, when a difficult or uncomfortable stage has been passed, he cannot really relax and it is when he does relax that he is so often more vulnerable. In a crew such as ours where the skipper is the centre of all expertise, the navigator, shipmaster and principal crew, he is not only under more load but it is more essential for him to stay alert. With a nominated mate who works in parallel, keeps the plot and sails the ship in his or her own right when the skipper is below, it is very different, but Joyce hadn't been asked to do any of those things and so she had steered the course ordered, fully trusting that I had weighed up all the odds.

Not that I was relaxing down there with my archaic spanners, but I was certainly not thinking about navigation. It was a fine day, but we were going to need the engine and that was uppermost in my mind. We were not steering dead into the tidal stream; we must have had it fine on our port bow and hence, as our speed fell, we remained with our bows pointing as ordered but sheering bodily to starboard.

How close we actually came to running on a spur of the Goodwin Sands I don't know, because we didn't take a sounding with the handlead, but judging by the sea state and those agitated fishermen – very close.

And so I end this collection as I began it – by coming very close to being yet one more victim of the Goodwins. Or perhaps becoming a victim of that arch enemy of all sailors, a blend of carelessness and relaxed vigil. A lot more water has passed under my keel since the last of these incidents happened, and being a good deal older I now tend to be over-cautious. And yet it is when I relax and find myself still taking it easy when I should be squinting around in some trepidation that I really get scared.

Index